DATE DUE

12 '97			

DEMCO 38-297

STORYTELLING

The Art and the Purpose

A Manual on How to Tell Stories
With Fifteen Typical Stories to Tell

by
LAURA S. EMERSON
Associate Professor of Speech,
Marion College, Marion, Indiana

Author and Compiler of
Twenty-five Inspiring Readings

Let me tell the stories,
and I care not who writes the textbooks.
— *Dr. Stanley Hall*

ZONDERVAN PUBLISHING HOUSE
GRAND RAPIDS   MICHIGAN

STORYTELLING
The Art and the Purpose
Copyright 1959 by
Zondervan Publishing House
Grand Rapids, Michigan

Library of Congress Catalog Number 59-14741

Printed in the United States of America

To
WILLIAM
who shared many a
story hour — enriching,
molding, and purposeful

INTRODUCTION

There is an important difference between reading stories aloud and telling them. It is better to read them well than to tell them poorly, but there are some which, when told effectively, provide for the child, and perhaps for the teller, an experience unique and wonderful. Some stories should be read and not told because they depend for their charm and meaning upon the words and style of the author. On the other hand, a significant area in the total experience of every child awaits the cultivation, the challenge, and the contribution of the qualified storyteller.

Part of the personal equipment for storytelling is a wide acquaintance with literature and people. Not many attempts have been made to bring together into one textbook the principles and practices which combine with this to effect the true art of storytelling. Those phases of the art which can be studied and cultivated by formal education are simply but effectively treated in this volume.

The author is qualified by personal traits, training, and experience to write such a volume. She was my teacher, both by precept and example, in the art of effective interpretation and communication of literature, especially the literature of the Bible. Recollections of her classes vie with my memories of earlier experiences in which parents and Sunday School teachers made the Great Book live through stories well told and lessons well taught.

I commend this volume to those who seek to prepare themselves to teach in the public schools, work in the field of religious education, and become the kind of parents who can contribute significantly to the growth of their children through the art of storytelling. In addition to the basic principles involved in recognizing a good story and preparing to tell it well, the reader will find valuable assistance in the author's suggestions of good story sources, her discussion of special program features related to storytelling, and the presentation of typical stories to tell.

MILO A. REDIGER
Vice President and Academic Dean,
Taylor University
Liberal Arts Study Coordinator,
North Central Association

PREFACE

Storytelling is an art meriting the best mastery of its basic techniques and foundation-principles. The Commonwealth Teacher's Training Study lists ability in storytelling as one of the skills a teacher should possess. Not only teachers benefit from a knowledge of this art, but also librarians, camp supervisors, religious educators, parents, and all those who seek to win children and influence their choices.

Because a child is "wax to receive and granite to retain," the story that stresses character development has been emphasized — the story with a purpose. A child is like a bank in which to deposit hard-earned wisdom and dreams for a better world. Storytelling should encourage him to guard those gems and invest them with a profit since he will soon be directing the affairs of men.

Although nearly everyone has been telling stories since he learned to talk, few are "born" but all are potential storytellers. Anyone with an earnest desire may acquire the art. Even the best of story craftsmen may disagree on method, but the underlying skills are the same. Nevertheless, there are some profitable "do's and don'ts" from the experiences of the storytellers of the past.

This book has grown out of many years of stimulating experiences with stories and students in college and youth camps. It is designed to aid the would-be storyteller in mastering his art by (1) cultivating an appreciation for the artistic and ethical values of a good story, by (2) knowing the steps in the preparation of a story for telling, and by (3) developing an individual charm in the telling. Since this text is slanted toward the classroom for the elementary teacher, suggestions for discussions, further reading, and class projects have been added at the end of each chapter.

We send forth this book with the hope that each of its readers may realize anew the joys of storytelling and may sense his dormant talents as a storyteller — the power to inspire and to satisfy both the mind and the spirit.

After working with children in India, Mrs. Bessie S. Ashton expressed the power of the storyteller in her poem, "The Heart of a Child":

> The heart of a child is a scroll,
> A page that is lovely and white;
> And to it as fleeting years roll,
> Come hands with a story to write.
>
> Be ever so careful, O hand;
> Write thou with a sanctified pen.
> Thy story shall live in the land
> For years in the doings of men.
>
> It shall echo in circles of light,
> Or lead to the death of a soul.
> Give here but a message of right,
> For the heart of a child is a scroll.

— LAURA S. EMERSON

Marion, Indiana
September, 1959

TABLE OF CONTENTS

PART II — FIFTEEN TYPICAL STORIES TO TELL

LIST OF CHARTS

Part I
How to Tell Stories

THE TEACHER

Lord, who am I to teach the way
To little children day by day,
So prone myself to go astray?

I teach them knowledge, but I know
How faint they flicker and how low
The candles of my knowledge glow.

I teach them power to will and do,
But only now to learn anew
My own great weakness through and through.

I teach them love for all mankind
And all God's creatures, but I find
My love comes lagging still behind.

Lord, if their guide I still must be,
Oh, let the little children see
The teacher leaning hard on Thee.

— LESLIE PINCKNEY HILL

Used by permission of the author.

cause it also reflects our appreciation of a tree. The painter uses a different medium for his expression, and like Corot, portrays the "Road through the Trees" in color. Passing by the pen or paintbrush, the musician uses tones of harmony and song. Regardless of the medium, each is an artist who interprets life as he senses and experiences it, then "pours in the oil and wine" that heals the listener.

Why is storytelling an art? According to Ruskin, the message which kindles fresh fires in our soul is not art unless it has three factors: truth, beauty, and the power to elevate and uplift. A story of purpose meets these artistic demands. The sensing and sharing of this vital truth that feeds the life of the spirit is creative. Curry understandingly taught, "Anything realized intensely becomes poetic. . . . Impression must always precede expression."

Before telling the story of the "Maid of Emmaus," the storyteller must saturate himself with the message Agnes Sligh Turnbull wished to share — the joy of sacrificial giving. He must sense the longing of the lonely, unloved girl until she met the Master, then picture the preparation of her love-gift and its presentation. When the message has become a very part of the warp and woof of his inner being, the storyteller artistically reproduces his personal story. It has become a work of art. Never confuse art with artificiality. Art is something felt, not assumed.

The Harvard committee, in their studies on general education, reported that the arts are "probably the strongest and deepest of all educative forces." Regarding this, Elizabeth Nesbitt has written:

> Storytelling recognizes the value of stimulus and response, the place of inspiration in true education. . . . It is an art which can broaden the horizon of ordinary men, which can give them the extent of their potential greatness. It is an art which reveals the common humanity of men, the instinctive belief in the worth and meaning of the human spirit. It is one method whereby the hearts and minds of children may be opened to the fact that the present stems from the past, that we of the new world share a common heritage with those of the old.[3]

[3]"The Art of Storytelling," *Horn Book* (December, 1945), Vol. XXI, No. 6, p. 442. Used by permission.

Who, then, may tell stories? Anyone may who goes questing for a message to share, who cultivates the elusive inner and spiritual graces, who loves life and people, and who loses self in the kindling of another's flame. This ability is recognized as dramatic instinct which consists of (1) imagination, the power to relive the situation, to see between the lines and visualize the picture; and (2) sympathy, the power to "other" yourself or put yourself in the place of the characters, sensing their joys and sorrows, motives and aspirations, successes and failures. Dramatic instinct gives the power to understand, then to transmit that knowledge to the listener.

When the philosophy for storytelling in the New York Public Library was adopted, storytellers were expected to have a wide knowledge of books, poise, dignity, warmth, and a love for sharing stories. Mary Gould Davis said, "Only training and experience can make storytelling effective. In branches where there is talent, judgment, poise to bring to the storytelling, the children listen and are satisfied. Where there is only limited power to interpret books, children are restless."[4]

Techniques may be taught, but living appreciations must be caught and felt. After the would-be storyteller absorbs a beautiful truth, he must study the skills and techniques of the art. This requires purpose, practice, and patience, before it can be perfected. To be able to paint words and ideals on the mental canvasses of the listeners is the delightful joy of the story artist.

STORYTELLING ARTISTS

A reference to the techniques of a few distinguished professional story-artists will be an encouragement to all would-be storytellers. Although their styles may differ, all possessed a message to transmit to others. At a recent national Storytelling Festival, a day was set aside to honor each of three story-artists: Ruth Sawyer, Gudrun Thorne-Thomsen, and Mary Gould Davis. Since much of the in-

[4]Augusta Baker, "More about Storytelling" (*Junior Libraries,* October, 1956), Vol. III, No. 2, p. 98. Used with permission.

centive to professional storytelling in the United States is
credited to Marie Shedlock, we shall speak of her first.

Marie Shedlock, noted English educator, visited in America where she promoted the story hour, particularly in
libraries. During the First World War she returned to this
country and spent five years traveling from Boston to San
Francisco telling her stories, especially those of Hans
Christian Andersen. Hers was a literary rather than a folk
art. Because she would not tamper with the words of
Andersen, she memorized them, characterizing subtly with
expansive gestures and flawless diction. A tiny woman with
a deep, resonant voice and dramatic quality, she charmed
her enormous audiences of young and old. Ruth Sawyer
lists the qualities that enthralled her listeners, proving her
the artist.[5]

Ruth Sawyer, famous American storyteller and writer,
credits her love of telling, writing, and listening to stories
to her Irish nurse, Johanna. This appreciation led her to
foreign countries to collect old tales from Ireland, Mexico,
and Spain. Her artistry is felt in the warmth and richness
of her tones and in the music and precision of her words.
Those who cannot hear her directly may listen to her recorded stories. "The Frog," a spiritualized tale of old Spain,
is an excellent example.[6] As a professional storyteller for
the New York Public Lecture Bureau, she skilfully practices
her art.

Gudrun Thorne-Thomsen, Norwegian-born teacher, in-
herited a love for the sagas of her own country which she
expressed in a lifetime of storytelling. "I have told stories
to children," she said, "from Canada to Southern California,
to children in Cuba and in the Hawaiian Islands. . . . Everybody loves them, old and young." She translated and
adapted the folk tales she had known as a child. She in-
structed the storytellers of the Cleveland Public Library
and of the Carnegie Library of Pittsburgh. A restrained
storyteller, she painted her pictures in a light, sweet, grave

[5]*The Way of the Storyteller* (New York: Viking Press, 1947), p. 127.
[6]These story records may be purchased from the American Library
Association, (50 East Huron St., Chicago 11, Illinois).

voice which captured her listeners at once. She stood quietly, rarely gesturing, developing her folk tales with simplicity and integrity of spirit and diction. Her stories have been recorded for the Library of Congress.[7]

Mary Gould Davis, eminent storyteller, also had an Irish nurse who incited an interest in the folklore of other lands. She worked with the children in the Brooklyn and the New York Public Libraries, sharing her rich gifts of storytelling. Six times she crossed the ocean to seek out the King Arthur legends, the Song of Roland, and the folk tales around the world.

Time would fail to tell of other artists who wore the storytellers's mantle — Carolyn Sherwin Bailey, Sara Cone Bryant, Anna Cogswell Tyler, Edna Lyman Scott, Lucine French, Richard T. Wyche, John Cronan, and William McGuffey. Dwight L. Moody, Charles Spurgeon, Henry Van Dyke, and Phillip Brooks were noted for the power of illustration and dramatic incident in their ministry. Each contributed lasting gifts to the storytelling art.

DISCUSSION SUGGESTIONS

1. What is art? What are the qualifications of an artist?
2. How do we apply the principles of art in everyday living?
3. Why are we justified in calling storytelling an art?
4. What is the secret of success of some untrained storytellers?
5. Explain the quotation from Curry at the beginning of the chapter.
6. What storytelling artists have you known?
7. How were stories used during the Middle Ages?
8. How are stories used by educators and religious leaders today?
9. Name a story which has fired your imagination.
10. How may you become an artist in storytelling?

STIMULATING READING

Sawyer, Ruth. *The Way of the Storyteller.* New York: Viking Press, 1947.
    I. "Storytelling — A Folk-Art"
   VII. "The Power of Creative Imagination"

[7]Ibid.

JOHNSON, GERTRUDE. *Studies in the Art of Interpretation.* New York: D. Appleton-Century Co., 1940.
    IV. "This Thing Called Dramatic" — Agnes Black
    IX. "Speech as a Fine Art" — Agnes Black
KUNITZ, STANLEY, and HAYCROFT, HOWARD (eds.). *The Junior Book of Authors.* New York: H. W. Wilson Co., 1951.

SUGGESTED PROJECTS

1. Listen to a story record by an artist.
2. Report on three storytellers from *The Junior Book of Authors.*
3. Listen to a radio story. Check the criteria of a children's broadcast given in Chapter VIII.
4. Contact your local branch of the National Story League for a storyteller.
5. Attend a library story hour.
6. Order a free reprint of Ruth Sawyer's *For the Storyteller* from Compton's Pictured Encyclopedia, F. E. Compton Co., 1000 North Dearborn St., Chicago 10, Illinois.

CHAPTER II

WHY TELL STORIES?

In order to teach a child truth, it is necessary to teach him fiction. — PLATO

Many centuries ago, a rich caliph in Bagdad gave a banquet in honor of the birth of his son. All the nobility who partook of the feast brought costly gifts — each one except a young sage named Mehelled Abi, who came empty handed. When he salaamed the caliph in greeting, he explained: "Since the young prince will receive many gifts of gold and jewels, I shall give him something more precious. Every day, from the time he is old enough to understand until he enters manhood, I will come to the palace and tell him the stories of our Arabian heroes. Then when he becomes our chief, he will be a just and merciful ruler."

Mehelled Abi kept his word. When the young prince finally became caliph, the fame of his good works spread throughout the land. Then his teacher inscribed on a scroll that is still to be seen in the Lichtenthal collection of manuscripts at Budapest, "It was because of the seed sown by the tales."

Just so, the storyteller today sows seeds of purpose which ripen into joy, knowledge, character, and conduct. The story becomes a universal tool with an inherent appeal to every age of every land.

THE PURPOSES OF STORYTELLING

Why do we tell stories? Ruth Sawyer answers this question by saying:

To be able to create a story, to make it live during the moment of the telling, to arouse emotions, . . . wonder, laughter, joy, amazement — this is the only goal a storyteller may have. To honor one's art. To hold for it an integrity of mind, a love and propensity for it. To build richly of experience into one's life that there may be more to give

out in the telling. To establish one's place in the fellowship
of spirit that there may be spiritual substance as well as
intellectual enjoyment in what is shared. To keep step with
a child's fancy, to abide for a little space in the Land of
Faery, to know joy unrestrained and those tender secret
longings that belong at the heart of childhood . . . these are
some of the markers along the way of the storyteller.[1]

Since we are creatures of emotion, intellect, and will or
personality, we tell stories that will appeal to, satisfy, and
influence these three characteristics. A definite goal adds
much to the success of the story. Edward Porter St. John,
in his *Stories and Storytelling*, gives seven aims of storytelling that suggest the purposes discussed here.

1. *Stories give pleasure.* "A good story," wrote Dr. Henry
Van Dyke, "is its own excuse for being." The child who
begs, "Tell me another story," reveals that the story has
made him happy and has satisfied his emotional hungers.
While a story may teach a lesson or relax a tense situation,
the primary purpose is for the enjoyment it brings. It is a
joyous reward of faithful endeavor — a part of the recreation hour.

A good story feeds the life of the spirit often emaciated
by materialistic influences. All great art appeals to the
growth of the spirit. G. Stanley Hall, the great educator,
knowingly wrote, "Stories are the natural soul-food of children, their native air and vital breath; but our children are
too often either story-starved or charged with ill-chosen or
ill-adapted twaddle tales."

I have seen the dark, pinched faces of little children in
Mexico City, as they gathered around the storyteller during
the Sunday school hour. As the story progressed, poverty-
stricken homes were forgotten; faces relaxed in smiles; eyes
lit up. They had glimpsed a better life, and their spirits were
refreshed.

Seumaus MacManus, Irish storyteller, says of storytelling:
The art carries with it and fosters community feeling, the
brotherhood of man, fireside magic, home influence, and
joy. . . . The storyteller is as the Promised Land, alluring,

[1]Ruth Sawyer, *The Way of the Storyteller* (New York: The Viking Press,
Inc., 1942), p. 148. Used by permission.

fruitful, joy-giving — his mind a blessed region flowing with milk and honey. The storyteller refreshes the weary, rejoices the sad, and multiplies the joy of those who are already glad. He is a God-gift to the community. Welcome him, nurture him, cherish him.[2]

2. *Stories develop the imagination.* For the younger child, the imagination is the chief means of training. Storytelling launches him into the world of make-believe which will help him to take the initiative in later life. Vicariously he translates the pictured ideals into action, seeing himself with the personal qualities of the hero. Whatever a child loves, he is potentially. James Stephens believed that "a leprechaun is of more value to the earth than is a Prime Minister."

What mother has not reminded little Johnny that if he wanted to be a soldier, he would march right off to bed. Because Johnny's desire to be his imaginary hero is greater than his dislike of bedtime, he goes without a struggle. It is understood that the ideals presented must be those which Johnny admires.

Walt Whitman recognized this psychological truth when he wrote:

There was a child went forth every day
And the first object he look'd upon, that
    object he became,
And that object became part of him for the
    day or a certain part of the day
Or for many years or stretching cycles of years.[3]

For almost ten years, Mrs. Marjorie Maddock of Chicago has been telling stories to the child wards of the Cook County Juvenile Court at the request of Judge Robert J. Dunne. This message-bringer felt rewarded when the superintendent told her that the children were talking about her stories and the characters in them. She recalled a recent incident when a small negro girl interrupted one of her stories to say, "Storyteller Miss, I'm not afraid now to see the judge. This morning Faith shined the lamp of Trust in my eyes."

2"Foreword," 1924-25 *Year Book,* National Story Teller's League. Used with permission of the author.
3*Leaves of Grass* (New York: Grosset & Dunlap), p. 119. Used with permission.

Adults as well as children want a quickening of the imagination. This picture-making faculty of the mind, which reveals the true relationship of things, transforms the work of the housewife, the businessman, and the schoolteacher. Walter Pitkin taught, "Assign to almost any task requiring thought an imaginative man with scant logic, and an unimaginative logician; nine times out of ten the former will handle it more successfully."

As we see and feel we come into understanding. The well-chosen story encourages sympathy, sociability, and warm-heartedness, brushing away any accumulated dust on our ideals. A mind fed only through the eye-gate is rarely stimulated to develop imagination or to read further. Mrs. Frank Clark Sayers, lecturer in storytelling at the University of California, senses today's need when she says:

> In an age when all the world's not a stage, but a screen, a picture, a delineation of the obvious object and the obvious symbol for emotion; in an age when the imagination is dulled and stunted by a surfeit of pictures in magazines, textbooks, billboards, busses, and newspapers; in an age when every hour of the day and night is filled with shadows of men and women moving fast, talking fast, lest they should lose their Hooper rating. In such an age, the art of the storyteller remains, giving his listeners the space, the time, and the words with which to build in their imaginations the "topless towers," "the stately pleasure domes," the shapes and sounds none knows nor hears save each mind for itself.[4]

3. *Stories illustrate unfamiliar truths.* While it is true that stories appeal greatly to the emotions, they also add to the general intellectual training. Children do not readily grasp abstract or symbolic ideas, but they can understand truth in concrete form. Knowledge of the world outside their own environment is gained through the experiences of others. "The telling of stories," wrote Friedrich Froebel, "refreshes the mind as a bath refreshes the body; it gives exercise to the intellect and its powers; it tests the judgment of the feelings."

Harrower taught that no ideas could become the perma-

[4]"From Me to You," *Junior Libraries*, (September, 1956), Vol. 3, No. 1, p. 3. Used with permission.

nent possession of the world which did not first enter through the door of childhood. What better example of a good neighbor could we have than the parable of the Good Samaritan, or of a shyster than Shakespeare's Shylock? Stories may inspire Christian attitudes and create a desire to give happiness to others through service.

For some time I have been telling stories from Christian biography in summer youth camps. Such incidents aid in making vocational choices. When a teen-ager stops to say, "I want to be like that doctor," we are aware again that noble lives incite nobility. The right story should prepare us for the battle of life with attitudes which make for pleasing personalities. We are reminded of the immortal words of Xavier, "Give me the children until they are seven and anyone may have them afterwards."

Psychologists also teach that by the time a child is seven he has received three-fourths of his education. Much of our knowledge of history, travel, customs, and countries, was first introduced in the story hour.

4. *Stories cultivate a taste for the best in literature.* The wise storyteller may select various stories which a child might not choose for himself or be able to understand. Many of the great epics can be presented in story form. Gladstone turned to Homer, and Fox and Lincoln to Shakespeare for stimulation. Storytelling should awaken an interest in the works of the best authors.

Great fiction provides a laboratory course in human nature. There is nothing like storytelling to launch a child into a new realm of understanding. Stories of the past reveal the genius of a people, not only the facts, but also their attitudes of mind and behavior. True education is an adjustment toward self, toward others, and toward God. Stories set the child to thinking and so fix his attitudes toward life.

The storyteller has an opportunity to present the finest literature to receptive young minds, to stimulate their perceptions through his sympathetic interpretations of the pathos, comedy, tragedy, hope, despair, and faith inherent in the stories he tells. He opens the door to the world of magic and make-believe, and he tells true stories of men and women who have overcome their own obstacles and found satisfying solutions to their own life problems. The master weaver of tales wields a tremendous power.[5]

5. *Stories improve language and vocabulary.* Hearing the best in literature will develop a growing power of aural comprehension. A word heard and understood is easier to recognize in print. Ruskin testified that he owed his artistic diction to his mother's insistence that he read a chapter from the Bible daily while she corrected his expression. As a child hears a good story, he desires to retell it, thus improving his own powers of expression in literary language.

It is stimulating to read Annis Duff's experiences in increasing children's vocabularies by having fun with words first introduced in stories. Dictionary study followed the discussion even in pre-school days.[6] With such a rich heritage of story-lore and language, the child learns to read more easily.

6. *Stories influence character and conduct.* "We are what we read," wrote John Wesley. The prophet Nathan used a story to show David his wrong. *Uncle Tom's Cabin* had much to do with stopping the spread of slavery. McGuffy adopted the story method to teach moral truths. Children assimilate long before they analyze. Centuries ago Socrates wrote: ". . . and shall we just carelessly allow children to hear any casual tales which may be devised by casual persons and to receive in their minds ideas for the most part the very opposite of those which we should wish them to have when they are grown up?"

In his study of belief, F. H. Lund asked a number of individuals to rate the sources of his belief. He found that teaching and training were greater determinants of belief than any other factor. Our beliefs are by-products of social influences.[7] He might have added that many of these beliefs are cultivated through stories.

The story becomes one of the most effective instruments in religious education. Children may see the inevitable working of God's laws, the triumph of right. Religious feel-

[5]Bess Porter Adams, *About Books and Children* (New York: Henry Holt and Co., 1953), p. 317. Used with permission.
[6]*Bequest of Wings* (New York: Viking Press, 1946), chap. VII, p. 81.
[7]F. H. Lund, "The Psychology of Belief," *Journal of Abnormal Psychology,* (April, 1925), Vol. 20, pp. 174-196.

ing is awakened. Reverence for God and His handiwork and ethical standards are established. Faith, understanding, and daily companionship with Christ may be implanted in a child from babyhood. He learns to discriminate between the false and the true so that he need not be lost in confusion.

While teaching in a junior high in a resort community, I once used the story of little Peter Billhorn who, when drowning, had clasped his hands tightly in prayer as he came up for the last time. This act enabled the men to rescue him by putting a pole under his hands. I thought no more of the story until a few months later, when one of my junior girls drowned during a vacation period. Those who saw her come up the last time said her hands were clasped in prayer, though she was not rescued. The story had made a lasting impression and incited faith.

Dr. J. Robertson McQuilkin tells of a recent survey of 5,000 Christian college students from all parts of the nation. He found that the most fruitful field of evangelism was among children and youth. One-half of those from non-Christian homes found Christ from 12-17 with 16 as the peak age; of Christian homes, one-third from 8-12 with a rapid decline after 12.[8]

Because a story makes such lasting impressions upon a child, it must be selected carefully from the great flood of fiction. A son accused of wasting his time with trashy stories said they didn't take up any room in his mind. His father asked him to bring a basket of apples. When this was done, he told the boy to empty the apples into the corner and fill the basket half full of chips. Wondering, the boy obeyed. "Now put the apples back into the basket," suggested the father. "But they won't go in when the basket is half full of chips," the boy protested. "That's the point," answered his father, "neither can you get your mind full of the things you are going to need to equip you for life when you already have it half full of cheap literature."

Dr. Ullin Leavell, director of the McGuffy Reading Clinic at the University of Virginia and author of a new series of public school textbooks, charges that in the stories of to-

[8]J. Robertson McQuilkin, "Born of the Spirit," *Christian Life*, (March, 1954), p. 26.

day's textbooks, "there is nothing to be remembered, no great lesson left for him to live by." Speaking to educators, he urged that religious principles without any sectarian slant be included in the textbooks. He emphasized eleven basic principles of "cooperation, courage, fairness, friendliness, honesty, kindness, patriotism, perseverance, responsibility, reverence, and unselfishness."

Every child is becoming what the man will be. William Dean Howells comprehended this truth when he wrote, "Men's work in making books is all in vain if books in turn do not make the man."

THE VALUES OF STORYTELLING

1. *A good story relaxes mental and nerve tensions.* Classroom atmosphere becomes more informal. As a statesman, Lincoln used anecdotes to tide over an otherwise stormy session. Happy attitudes produce greater responses. How true it is that whatever you make a child love and desire is more important than what you make him learn. I have found a story a valuable help to concentration after a recess period of strenuous activity.

2. *A story forms habits of attention.* Storytellers hope for voluntary attention even though it is an effort and children listen to be polite. Of greater importance is spontaneous attention without conscious effort — that concentration that results from intense interest.

3. *Stories establish a sympathetic relationship* between teacher and pupil or mother and child. The companionship of stories belongs only to congenial souls. The spontaneous chuckle shared in common experiences will help to bring better cooperation with the teller's suggestions. When entering a classroom of youngsters as a new teacher, I invariably used an anecdote or story to orient myself with the pupils and to bring about an understanding relationship.

4. *Stories may serve as a disciplinary measure.* Instead of sending a child to the corner to think of ugliness or revenge, use a story of the boy who wanted to make things right. The child will want to be like the hero. A wise mother I knew, often made up a story when her children were quarreling — a story which shamed them into a better attitude.

Order may thus be restored in a roomful of restless children on a rainy day or on the playground. A humorous story often oils the pedagogical machinery.

The teacher with a fund of good stories on hand holds the key to any classroom situation. He has a story to make an ethical point when a problem arises. He can often solve a dispute or quiet an argument with the right story. He can bring laughter into his room. He knows that if he has a story to tell he can always relieve tension, fear, anger, or whatever emotion may occasionally disrupt his class; and, important to him, he recognizes the value of the story in establishing a happy relationship with his group, which carries beyond the story period to color all the classroom activities.[9]

DISCUSSION SUGGESTIONS

1. Why should the giving of joy be the first purpose of a story?
2. How may a story be used to combat juvenile delinquency?
3. Why do adults appreciate stories?
4. What is the importance of the story to the religious educator?
5. Explain Plato's statement at the beginning of this chapter.
6. Show how we are the "result of what we feed upon."
7. In what different situations have you seen stories used?
8. What story made a deep impression on you, and why?

STIMULATING READING

SMITH, ALPHONSO. *What Can Literature Do for Me.* New York: Doubleday, Doran & Co., Inc., 1931.

    I. "It Can Give You an Outlet"
    II. "It Can Keep before You the Vision of the Ideal"
    III. "It Can Give You a Better Knowledge of Human Nature"
    IV. "It Can Restore the Past to You"
    V. "It Can Show You the Glory of the Commonplace"
    VI. "It Can Give You the Mastery of Your Own Language"

SUGGESTED PROJECTS

1. Report on one of the chapters in Smith's book.
2. Hold a round-table discussion on the purposes of storytelling.
3. Name several stories which would accomplish each of the purposes of storytelling discussed in this chapter.
4. Tell a fable or anecdote that illustrates some abstract principle.
5. Relate a personal incident which might be used in teaching.

[9]Bess Porter Adams, *About Books and Children* (New York: Henry Holt and Co., 1953), p. 317. Used with permission.

CHAPTER III

WHICH STORY SHALL I TELL?

The more they know of heroes the more of heroes they will become. — CHARLEMAGNE

Of the writing of children's stories, there is no end. Out of this annual avalanche of fiction, how shall we select the right story for the particular listener at that specific moment? It is not enough to choose a story which interests him and influences his character. The purposeful story must also be appropriate for that particular occasion, hour of day, and the experiences of the group.

Some of the first questions I invariably ask when requested to tell a story are: "What age bracket is represented?" "What are their interests?" "Is the story to be told on the playground, at a party, or in the church?" One specialist with juniors whom I know, keeps a picture scrapbook of the traits and activities of junior boys and girls, that she may better understand them.

Four factors should be considered as a basis for the selection of the appropriate story: (1) the listener, (2) the literary quality of the story, (3) the storyteller, and (4) the library facilities.

THE LISTENER

A knowledge of the psychology of the child in the audience is a most important factor to consider in choosing the story. A story which fascinates a seven-year-old may have no appeal for his teen-age brother. Age, however, is not as great a concern as the stage of progress or the associations that a listener may bring to the story hour. What store of ideas are in his mind? What experiences other than at home? What stories does he already know?

The gift of selection comes to those who "learn" children before they try to teach them. The gap between the familiar and the unfamiliar must be bridged before the story is

33

PERIODS OF CHILD STUDY*

Dr. Clarence H. Benson

CHARACTER- ISTICS	INFANCY	EARLY CHILDHOOD	MIDDLE CHILDHOOD	LATER CHILDHOOD	EARLY ADOLESCENCE	LATER ADOLESCENCE
Physical	Actor	Player	Hustler	Rover	Change	Achievement
Mental	Discoverer	Questioner	Observer	Investigator	Criticism	Power
Social	....	....	....	Gangster	Companionship	Friendship
Spiritual	Imitator	Believer	Discriminator	Worshiper	Conversion	Instability

* From An Introduction to Child Study by Clarence H. Benson (Chicago, Illinois: The Bible Institute Colportage Association, 1935), Chapters IX - XIV. Used with permission.

CHART I

comprehended. Henry Ward Beecher once made the statement that a preacher could know the Bible from cover to
cover, and yet be unsuccessful in his field if he did not
understand people. This is also true of the storyteller.

The elementary or the Sunday School teacher usually has
the advantage over other storytellers in that the listeners
have similar ages and interests. If they are a heterogeneous
group, it is better to slant the story toward the older children. Sometimes the younger listeners may be dismissed
after the first story, the older ones remaining for the stories
appropriate for them.

Some stories can be appreciated by every age. A story
unsuited to the child in his period of development is not
a good one because he receives no message. There is no
exact time when one story interest ends and another begins.
Psychologists have identified the various periods of child
development and interest. Clarence Benson, who pioneered
in the field of child psychology especially for religious educators, classified each of the age groups according to physical, mental, social, and spiritual characteristics. Storytellers
may profit by examining his study. (See Chart I).

Although excellent classified storytelling lists are available
in literary and library references, every storyteller will want
to collect a personal repertoire. Therefore it is not our purpose to include a list of the many stories, but rather to
discuss (1) the characteristics of the age group, (2) the
story interests of each, and (3) examples that illustrate.
Each period is identified by its storytelling characteristic.

The Rhythmic Period — Pre-school Age.

Characteristics — The first years of a child's life are most
important in the formation of attitudes and habits of life.
His social and spiritual behavior patterns are being molded.
This is an age of physical activity when the child has many
muscles to wiggle with and only one to sit still. Much of the
time he plays alone with his own pets and toys. He is self-
centered around his familiar life at home. Curious about his
surroundings, he learns by touching, tearing and tasting until
he discovers for himself the world around him. He concen-
trates only a few minutes. A great imitator, he beats time,

folds his hands, and mimics those he sees. Attitudes of obedience, sharing, and worship are formed during this plastic period. It is only a step from interest in parents and other children to an awakening of God-consciousness and the loving care of a Heavenly Father.

Story interests — Since the child's attention span is brief, he wants "here and now" stories while he takes his bath or gets ready for a nap. He is happy sitting beside you or on your lap, looking at the picture book while you tell the story. His favorite characters are the family, animals, pets, and the familiar postman, groceryman, and garage attendant. They must be doing something all the time — the cat running away with the spoon or the gingerbread man whirling down the road. He prefers the tale to the story as he is not yet ready for the mechanics of plot. In his simple vocabulary, he likes action verbs, jingles, rhyme, and rhythm. He listens for the repetition of pleasant, rippling word sounds as found in alliteration and refrains. "I'll huff and I'll puff and I'll blow your house in," brings a delightful response from the favorite "The Three Little Pigs." He wants his stories told again and again — and in the same words.

If we want children to learn to love literature, we must help them to begin with the nursery rhymes. There is magic in the name of Mother Goose, who knew her child psychology when she told of happy and contrary, and of wise and simple children who run, play, eat, and sleep as in a child's world. There is only one Simple Simon as in the law of averages. Wise animals frolic. We don't know the origin of these rhymes, though Bostonians point to the headstone of Mary Goose in the Old Granary Burying Ground.

The simple folk tales abound with animals, repetition, and action. After telling the story of "The Three Billy-Goats Gruff" to a three-year-old in a home where I was visiting, I was asked again and again to tell of those "goats gruff," not a new story. The repetition, the animals, and the sense of justice were completely satisfying. "Henny Penny," "The Three Bears," "The Three Pigs," and "The Gingerbread Man," suggest the traditional favorites. To these may be added Beatrix Potter's *Tale of Peter Rabbit* and Wanda

Gag's *Millions of Cats,* each with expressive illustrations that have charmed the children of the last quarter century.

Bible stories never cease to fascinate. Choose those about the Good Shepherd, Noah and the Ark with all the animals, and the Baby Moses. And what story could hold more wonder and charm than that of the Angels and the Shepherds and the Baby Jesus? All of these are an essential part of every child's spiritual heritage.

The Inquisitive Period — Early Childhood

Characteristics — Now that the child is in school, he has learned to play with others. When he meets other children, he asks simple questions: "Who are you?" "Where do you live?" "What do you play?" Such spontaneous remarks reveal his broader range of interests. This is his sensory period. The key-word is change. Concerned with everyday things, he plays doctor, nurse, teacher, preacher, and driver. Inquisitive about his own little world, he asks countless questions which must be answered. "What makes the car go?" "Where does the wind come from?" "Who is God?" He is a veritable question mark. His interests now include the neighbors and what others say, think, and do. He believes what he is told. This is an age of great faith.

Story-Interests — The storyteller finds this child eager, responsive, and quite candid in his reactions to the story hour. Interested in the familiar still, he wants to hear of other children in far away lands. Curious about nature and animals, he likes stories that teach him about their habits, or that personify animals. He likes live creatures. Mechanized heroes as ships, fire engines, trains, and bulldozers satisfy his inquisitive nature. Simple plots and vivid sensory words appeal to him. One librarian tells of a boy who came daily to see the picture book illustrating a bull chasing a boy. When asked why he liked it, he explained, "I want to see if the boy has been caught yet!"

In the familiar "Bremen Town Musicians" we find many appeals to the senses, personified animals, and a repetition of plot. Rudyard Kipling's classic *Jungle Book* with the tales of "Rikki-Tikki-Tavi," and Knight's *Lassie Come Home* are stories of real animals. The story of "The Little Engine

That Could" or "The Three Freight Trains Take Their Loads to the City," picture mechanized heroes and are both informative and character-building. The Bible stories of creation, and of our first parents in Paradise, will answer many questions of young minds. Add the story of the boy Samuel, the shepherd boy David, and the little lame prince, Mephibosheth. Christmas and Easter stories help to establish attitudes of right and wrong, and encourage faith.

The Imaginative Period — Middle Childhood

Characteristics — This is the motor rather than sensory period — the age of make-believe when the child is on the border line of the realistic and the symbolic. Now he plays easily with others — boys with boys and girls with girls — each content with a voluntary segregation. He has acquired many useful skills. Keenly observant, he is gaining new concepts in terms of the old. He discriminates between right and wrong, and precept and practice. We are reminded of the time Tommy was sent from the table to wash his hands. "Haven't I always told you to wash your hands before eating?" his mother asked. "Once you didn't," remembered Tommy. "Train up a child in the way he should go, and once in a while walk there yourself," admonished Sam Jones.

Story-Interests — With a highly developed imagination, this child thinks in terms of the fanciful and the abstract. He lives on a magic carpet of kings and castles, fairy godmothers and seven-league boots. Animals are endowed with intelligence. Stories must be rich in sense appeals and uphold the truths of loyalty, kindness, and justice. Beside the simple folk tales, he likes Indian legends, the fables of Aesop of ancient Greece, and stories of hobbies and crafts.

The fairy tales are now as beloved as Mother Goose. As Kate Douglas Wiggin has put it: "Some universal spiritual truth underlies the really fine old fairy tale." The eternal truth of "Sleeping Beauty" teaches love's supreme power to awaken — the triumph over sleep, apathy, and death. Ruth Sawyer's Spanish story of "The Frog" stresses God's sovereignty. The incomparable stories of Hans Christian Andersen, of "Rip Van Winkle," of "Br'er Rabbit" in *Uncle*

Remus, The Adventures of Pinocchio, Alice in Wonderland, and Hawthorne's *Wonder Book* are best appreciated in this period. Among more recent favorites are the adventures of the small, hand-carved, wooden doll related in *Hitty: Her First Hundred Years,* and the experiences of the Indian girl in *Chi-Wee.*

The natural craving for flights of fancy is satisfied in the stories of the supernatural in the Bible. Best of all they are true — the pillar of cloud, the crossing of the Red Sea, and the sweetening of the waters of Marah. The miracles of the New Testament, the feeding of the 5,000, the healing of blind Bartimaeus, and the calming of the stormy waters — all help to establish a belief in the omnipotence of God. Boys and girls accept the story of Jonah and the big fish where they would challenge it should it first be told to them in their adolescent period. Presented sympathetically at this age, the story lays a cornerstone of faith.

The Heroic Period, Later Childhood

Characteristics — In contrast to the imaginative period, this is the realistic junior age. The key-word is energy — physical prowess. Juniors are alert, adventurous, self-reliant, and lovers of nature and the out-of-doors — the "Big Injun Age!" It is a time of health and hardihood. Follow the directions carefully for this recipe for preserving juniors:

    1 large grassy field
    ½ dozen children
    2 or 3 small dogs
    a pinch of brook and pebbles

Mix children and dogs well together and put them in field, stirring constantly. Pour brook over pebbles; sprinkle field with flowers; spread over a deep blue sky and bake in the sun. When brown, remove and set to cool in a bathtub.[1]

The quest for knowledge leads many a hopeful young scientist to take apart his watch or the old car. Mechanical interests are high. Ninety per cent of the children of this period are collectors. It is the golden age of memory when twice as much of the story is remembered as in the imag-

[1]Clarence Benson, *An Introduction to Child Study* (Bible Institute Colportage Association), p. 150. Used with permission.

inative period. The child has mastered the art of reading and finds pleasure in books. Mentally alert, he asks for the truth. Now the boy or girl is conscious of a social nature. True, he dislikes the opposite sex, but he shows a tendency to organize. He is fiercely loyal to his gang in the sense that he likes teamwork and wants to be with his own group. He greatly admires and seeks to imitate his heroes from both stories and life. As a hero-worshipper he recognizes authority, sensing God's right to rule the world as well as his life.

Benson refers to the university professor who resigned from teaching his Sunday school class of college men to teach junior boys. When asked why, he explained, "If you wanted to write your name on a brick, would you do it before or after it was baked?"

Story-Interests — Choose vigorously realistic stories from nature, science, and biography. Channel interests into historical narrative, legendary tales of Greece and Rome, classical myths, and explanations of how things work. Today there are excellent stories about birds, trees, chemistry, ships, planes, and adventure. Hawthorne's story of *The Great Stone Face* symbolizes the desire of each to be like his ideal. Frank Buck's *Bring Them Back Alive* tells of his capture of animals for zoos. Herman Hagedorn's *Book of Courage* portrays heroes in various vocations. There are many sources about heroes of the Old World, the American frontier, explorers, missionaries, inventors, and statesmen. The Bible stories of David and Goliath, Daniel in the Lion's Den, Barak, Gideon, Samson, Elijah, Nebuchadnezzar — in fact the first sixteen books of the Old Testament, omitting *Ruth,* teach ideals and patterns of noble living.

The Romantic Period — Early Adolescence

Characteristics — Adolescence is the epic period of high idealism which forms a bridge between the child and the adult. Under physical, emotional, and social tensions, his responses are often unpredictable. His likes and dislikes vary frequently. His rapid growth makes him awkward and easily embarrassed. He seeks justification for the whys and wherefores of life. It is not enough to be told to do things. Conscious of the opposite sex, he craves companionship. He may be advised, but not driven. This is the age of spiritual awakening and choice of lifework.

Story-Interests — Because of the high idealism of this age, story interests center around those who conquer circumstances through idealism and spiritual courage rather than physical valor. Select high-minded romance and adventure that show the true meaning of love, manhood, and womanhood. Legendary hero tales of King Arthur and his knights — Sir Galahad "whose strength was as the strength of ten because his heart was pure" — portray chivalry, adventure, and loyalty. Adapt Spenser's *Faery Queen* and Bunyan's *Pilgrim's Progress* and *Holy War*. The conquering of Mt. Everest and the martyrdom of the five missionaries to the Auca Indians challenge and inspire service today. The popularity of Grace Livingston Hill's books illustrates the desire for idealism. Choose the Biblical stories which deal with soul struggles as of Saul and David, David and Jonathan, Ruth, Esther, the calling of the disciples, and of Paul's conversion. The life of Christ is full of incidents that help to integrate personality and to transform the heart.

THE LITERARY QUALITY OF THE STORY

"Great stories brought to life by a great artist, like great music, belong to the whole world." The stories may be old, but the children are ever new! When outstanding persons were asked, "What book, other than the Bible, made the greatest impression on you as a child?" each named some story of literature: President Eisenhower, *Connecticut Yankee in King Arthur's Court;* Eddie Cantor, *Alice in Wonderland;* Billy Graham, *The Adventures of Marco Polo;* Helen Keller and Bernard Baruch, *Oliver Twist;* and Kate Smith, *Little Women.*[2]

All great literature is characterized by (1) truth and (2) beauty. While all stories may not be true to life, they must be true to truth and to principle. Even folk tales with personified animals may meet this standard. Grimm and Andersen teach contentment and modesty. Hans Christian Andersen's autobiographical "The Ugly Duckling," is allegorical

[2]"My Most Memorable Childhood Book," *Better Homes & Gardens,* (December, 1957), Vol. 35, No. 12, p. 8.

in that it portrays the misunderstood, humble creature who is finally recognized for his goodness.

A child demands a sense of justice in his stories. He wants to see right rewarded and wrong punished. Dr. Henry Van Dyke taught, "Never tag a moral to a story and never tell a story without a meaning." Human interest stories which affect the human soul have a permanence of appeal.

Beauty of style to the child means words of imagery and sense appeal that arouse intense interest and feeling. As George Henry Lewes puts it, "The child must feel before it can know; and knowledge, great and glorious as it is, can never be the end of life: it is but one of the many means." A good story has suspense as to the outcome. The older the listener, the more he wants to know the incentive behind the deeds of the characters. Action and movement, repetition, direct discourse, simplicity and conflict — these are all a part of good style. According to Ruskin, great style and great subject matter will have power to elevate. Since none but the best is good enough for the child, take time to tell the best, and comic books will lose their flavor.

Good literature for children is not something separate and far removed from the great body of literature enjoyed by adult readers. The same criteria apply to all literature. Good literature, whether for old or young readers, bears the mark of truth and integrity; it carries the reader along into genuine, if vicarious, experience; it stirs his emotions, arouses his curiosity, stimulates his mind, and gives him a measuring stick for living. The characters in the stories are as real as the people he knows; the ideas in essays, novels, plays, and poems are as true as the best thinking of the human mind.[3]

The Storyteller

In an examination I once asked what was meant by "possessing a story." One of the girls wrote regarding her father, a good storyteller: "When Daddy tells a story you can be sure he first liked it. 'It tickled his gizzard.' It struck a note with his personality and he saw the point. He already understood it. He grew in sympathy with it. He never tells a story that he cannot put himself into."

[3]Bess Porter Adams, *About Books and Children* (New York: Henry Holt & Co., 1953), p. vii. Used with permission.

Attitude — The spirit of the story must fit the teller's own mood. If we are not sympathetic and do not accept the truth of the story, we will find it hard to convince our listeners. Our own joyous animation and energetic enthusiasm will help to sell the story, for we are a salesman of ideals. "There is, after all," says Grant Overton, "only one test of a story — the test of what it makes you feel." If the story does nothing for us, it will do nothing for the listeners. We must feel that the story contains truth for us as well as for the boys and girls. If we are reasonably sure that we can bring the chosen story to life and by our own power recreate it, we have selected wisely. It goes without saying that our own ideals will be an example. We must have religious convictions before we can strengthen God-consciousness and reverence for the Creator in our listeners.

Expression — Wanda Gag refers to the "intimate me-to-you" quality of Grimm's tales in the original. This is the interpretation which listeners must sense in a storyteller. Gudrun Thorne-Thomsen possessed a sympathetic, creative quality which made her stories live. After hearing her, a six-year-old child put a small hand on her knee and asked softly, "Were you there?" How such rapport is revealed in voice and manner is developed further in Chapter VI.

Personal appearance — Children respond better when the storyteller's clothing is neat, becoming, and often colorful. A hat appears too formal for the homey art of storytelling. Bangles, brilliants, or anything that detracts from the message of the story are unessential. Katherine D. Cather tells of a playground story-teller who arrived in a gypsy costume and was immediately surrounded by a curious group. Missionary costumes of foreign lands often add to atmosphere.

Library Facilities

Naturally, story selections are limited to available sources. In order to have a worth-while story that suits both you and the listener, you will probably want to make your own collection of stories. By carefully culling church periodicals and educational magazines, you may discover often unused but valuable stories.

I have two scrapbooks — one of general purpose stories,

and one of stories especially for religious education, classified according to subject matter. These plus anthologies and
literary selections are readily available without a lot of
breathless searching. As storytellers we will want to keep
on the lookout for worth-while stories which we can possess
and transmit to others. See Bibliography.

DISCUSSION SUGGESTIONS

1. Must a story be "true to life"?
2. At what period do boys and girls begin to show different
   story preferences?
3. What qualities should a literary story for children possess?
4. How does the storyteller's mood affect the story hour?
5. Does time of day or location affect story choice?
6. Why should a storyteller understand the story interests of a
   child?
7. How can you cultivate an appreciation for the best in literature?

STIMULATING READING

SHEDLOCK, MARIE. *The Art of the Storyteller*
   IV. "Elements to Avoid in Selection of Material"
   V. "Elements to Seek in the Choice of Material"
SAWYER, RUTH. *The Way of the Storyteller*
   IX. "The Art of Selection"
ADAMS, BESS PORTER. *About Books and Children.* New York:
 Henry Holt & Co., 1953.
   Chapters V - IX
BENSON, CLARENCE. *An Introduction to Child Study*
   Chapters IX - XIII

SUGGESTED PROJECTS

1. Compile a list of stories appropriate for each period.
2. Talk with children about their story preferences.
3. Report on the psychology of the child in one period of
   development.
4. Visit the children's room in the library and observe the
   favorite books.
5. Begin a scrapbook of your own favorite stories for telling.
6. Make a personal bibliography of stories of folklore, biography, holiday, and religious education emphasis.
7. Make a list of fifteen good authors of children's stories, both
   old and new.

CHAPTER IV

WHAT IS A STORY?

He cometh unto you with a tale which holdeth children from play, and old men from the chimney corner.
— SIR PHILIP SIDNEY

Just as in the science laboratory we break up a chemical into its various elements in order to understand it, so we should analyze the different parts of a story. By studying its structure, we will be able to tell it more effectively and to learn what makes a story a work of art.

All great stories are alike in structure. The "Cinderella" theme is found in 345 variants in practically every racial group. Annie Moore lists only six dominant story patterns in the folk tales.[1] Various critics have suggested that the general plot classifications range from four to thirteen.[2] Professor John Milton Berdan of Yale University once tried an experiment to prove that the merits of a story depend more upon treatment than upon plot. He sent the same plot to fourteen noted writers asking for a story. Their stories were so varied in solution as to include almost every known type.[3]

DEFINITION OF THE STORY

Artistically, a story is hard to define because it is essentially a growing structure — a work of art with a message of beauty, truth, and power. It is an interpretation of life so sympathetically portrayed that it arouses intense interest and feeling. Through imagination, conflict, suspense, and movement, the story creates a sense of reality which sways the listener and feeds his spirit.

Technically, a story is more than a narrative or recital of

[1] *Literature Old and New for Children* (New York: Houghton Mifflin Co., 1934), p. 98.

[2] J. Berg Esenwein, *Writing the Short Story* (New York: Noble and Noble, 1928), p. 76.

[3] *Fourteen Stories from One Plot* (New York: Oxford University Press, 1932).

events. According to Emma Bolennis, a story is "the disentangling of a complicated situation, so that a single definite effect is made."[4] J. Berg Esenwein wrote: "A short-story is a brief, imaginative narrative, unfolding a single predominating incident and single chief character, by means of a plot, the details of which are so selected, and the whole treatment so organized, that a single impression is produced."[5] Both of these authorities recognized that the well-constructed story must be an organic whole.

This unified whole does not come about by accident. The story structure must reveal how a character meets a test. There must be (1) a brief setting, or time and place for the events to follow. (2) The character meets a test. He wants something difficult to obtain, and tries again and again to solve his problem, but fails. This struggle makes up (3) the conflict or plot. How the character overcomes the obstacle completes the story. All these experiences produce only one definite impression.

Although alike in structure, adult stories are developed with a more complicated mechanism than children's. The story for the child is simple and straightforward in its devices. Good must always be rewarded and bad punished. The beginnings are more direct and the endings final. The younger the child, the less complicated the situation. Boys and girls of the Rhythmic Period like the tale, the simple narrative that has no real plot, but continues from incident to incident with no essential change upon the characters. The omission or addition of another scene would not affect the outcome.

The Beginning of the Story

Just as first impressions are often lasting in meeting a person, so the opening sentences determine whether or not the story will hold interest. Shakespeare said of his players: "By their entrances and exits, shall they be known." The setting presents (1) the predominating character, (2) his conflict, and (3) the atmosphere or mood of the story. The questions, Who? Where? When? and Why? are answered in the introductory sentences or paragraphs.

[4]*Teaching Literature in the Grammar Grades and High School* (New York: Houghton Mifflin Co., 1929), p. 187.
[5]J. Berg Esenwein, op. cit., p. 30.

A track star who had successfully won the one-hundred-yard dash was asked how he attained such a record. He explained, "I practiced starting and running the first ten yards ten thousand times. I trained all my muscles just right so I could start at a bang!" Just as careful personal disciplining in beginning each story will help to create spontaneous attention.

I remember my own chagrin at a camp when asked to tell a story the second part of the period. On a hot day in a large tent with people passing, the first storyteller announced, "I'm waiting until you are all quiet so I can hear a pin drop. Your parents expect you to listen." As the group fidgeted in the heat, she continued, "I can't start until you are all quiet. I am waiting." Needless to say, the children were not eager to hear any story.

Begin at the latest possible moment as close to the conclusion as possible, rather than leisurely tuning up as an orchestra before a concert. Stories are often ruined at the first by a rambling beginning. Set the stage, draw back the curtain, and get into action. The first words must command and demand an attention that sends the mind leaping forward in expectation.

Avoid vague beginnings that lose attention. Contrast the approach in these two beginnings:

Once we decided to have a picnic so Uncle Jack and Aunt Sue got out the old Ford. I like a Chevrolet much better. Then they found they had a flat tire. I wanted to tell you about the lunch. I like hamburgers, but they all wanted weiners. Well, after we were all ready to start, et cetera.

*   *   *

I was eating a sandwich by the lake when I heard Jim call, "Help! Help!"

The long explanation of the first lulls to sleep rather than arousing curiosity. Why not come directly to the purpose of the story?

Use the flashback. In introducing the problem, it is not necessary to give the entire life story of the hero. After creating interest through a striking incident, bring in the needed information from his past by a few well-chosen sentences of explanation. The old Roman storytellers used the phrase, *"In media res"* (in the middle of things), and plunged into the conflict, filling in the background as the story progressed. By a descriptive word, gesture, or tone, the atmosphere can be so established that it relives in the imagination of the listener.

This pattern is usually followed in the biographical story. After picturing the character in action in some high point of his career, his chronological facts may later be woven into the story.

Keep suspense by suggesting, not foretelling the outcome. The storyteller who begins, "I want to tell you a story about a brave boy named David who killed the big giant with a stone from his sling," has stolen the meat from the dish. He leaves little to feed the imagination. The listener has already drawn the shades of his mind.

Study the beginnings of the best stories. Note their brevity, their directness in portraying mood, in revealing character, and in suggesting the issues involved. Bible narratives are excellent patterns:

＊　＊　＊

In those days was Hezekiah sick unto death.

＊　＊　＊

A sower went forth to sow.

＊　＊　＊

Now it came to pass in the days when the Judges ruled, that there was a famine in the land.

＊　＊　＊

Now Naaman, captain of the host of the king of Syria, was a great man with his master, and honourable, because by him the Lord had given deliverance unto Syria: he was also a mighty man in valour, but he was a leper.

＊　＊　＊

When the mind asks, "What will happen?" the beginning is a provocative one. Keep the listeners participating in the action from the very first. Sense the expectancy in these stories:

> Once upon a time there was a little White Rabbit with two beautiful long pink ears and two bright red eyes and four soft little feet — such a pretty little White Rabbit, but he wasn't happy.
> "The Little Rabbit Who Wanted Red Wings"
> — *Southern Folk Tale*

＊　＊　＊

An old clock that had stood for fifty years in a farmer's kitchen without giving its owner any cause of complaint, early one morning, before the family was stirring, suddenly stopped.
"The Discontented Pendulum" — *Jane Taylor*

❖   ❖   ❖

There was sorrow in heaven!
"Out of the Ivory Palaces" — *J. H. Hunter*

❖   ❖   ❖

A native runner came down from the hills and sank on John Steadman's doorstep.
"White man, he die."
"Ellis dead? Why, he's just been here six weeks. How? How did he die?"

"No One Cares — Why Should We?" — *Grace Sanders*

❖   ❖   ❖

INTRODUCTIONS

The storyteller may often want to give a personal introduction to the story before the actual beginning. Some stories as "The Shining Secret" and "The Boy Handel"[6] include their own familiar setting. Tell your listeners just enough that they will be with you imaginatively in the very first sentence.

Orient listeners by starting with some known incident or reference which will prepare them for the story. This is especially necessary to freshen an old familiar story. For the Rhythmic Period with the story of Creation, you might begin with the season — the first day of spring or winter. Ask the children to see, hear, and smell the season which is appropriate. Suggest that all didn't just happen, but was made according to a plan. Then you are ready to say that, "In the beginning God created," et cetera.

Picture something happening with the listeners as participants. In this way you almost sneak in the back way to the story, but are bound to hold interest. Picture mother's room on sewing day — the paper pattern, the following of directions for the dress. Boys who model airplanes, also follow a pattern. By talking about familiar patterns, you are ready to present patterns in the Old Testament, and the story of Noah's Ark for an older group who have heard the animal approach from babyhood.

[6]See Part II.

Stories with a foreign setting or historical background may be clarified with a few brief remarks. "Once upon a time" or "Long, long ago," locates a fairy story in time. Older groups may want to know whether it is an Irish, German, or English folk tale. Adults often like a reference to the author. "When Indians roamed our country," or, "Fifty years ago," is better than giving the actual date. Stories of a Biblical theme may be introduced by "When Jesus was on earth," or "And it came to pass." This phrase is also preserved by Marie Shedlock in her versions of the old myths of India.

It is only fair to a listener that he know whether the story is true or not. One storyteller pretended she had a bag of stories over each shoulder and asked her listeners whether they wanted a "true" or a "let's suppose" story. This distinction is particularly necessary if a story hour includes fairy, historical, and Bible stories.

The Body of the Story

The main part of the story consists in the "disentangling of a complicated situation." This sequence of events is maintained by (1) action, (2) suspense, (3) directness, and (4) climax.

Action. After you "get ready, set, and go" as the track runner, keep the action moving in a series of connected incidents. Each episode should contribute something to the following one until the climax is reached. This movement should be orderly, incident by incident, anticipating the high peak but not revealing it in advance. The action of the story may not always be a physical struggle, as with David and Goliath. It may be between man and nature as when Christ calmed the storm, or the mental and spiritual conflict of the prayer in Gethsemane.

Suspense. Capitalize on the surprise element throughout the whole story. Picture just enough hazards to keep the listeners waiting and wondering how the story will turn out. It is this element of suspense which produces rapt attention. Obstacles must be overcome, choices made, and problems solved in the well-constructed story. If the struggle is too obvious or weak, the suspense is tame. There is no dramatic appeal. Lead the hero from crisis to crisis until the listeners wonder if he ever can extricate himself, and if he does, how. (Note chart II in the next chapter.)

I recall drawing near the climax of a story, with the last hurdle to be met, when a ten-year-old boy jumped up interrupting, "Aw, I knew it would turn out that way." He sat down without disturbing the others also lost in the story, and I continued to the end. When the true climax was reached and the hero succeeded as he had hoped, he sighed with relief.

Directness. Keep the story progressing without side trips or episodes. Children like a straight-ahead course requiring little explanation or detail. Move swiftly without a break. When Kipling encountered a tangent to the main plot, he would subtly suggest, "But that is another story." Rarely is it wise to ask the children questions or allow them to interrupt with questions during the telling of the story. Irrelevant remarks such as, "Is the hour over? Mother said I must come home in an hour," are sure to impede the story build-up.

One lawyer said he could test a logical mind by noting the effect of this incident: "Two boys were chasing a rabbit which finally ran under the barn floor. Just then a fire-siren blew, and the boys rushed off to the fire. After an exciting afternoon they hurried home for lunch, sharing the events of the day." Unless the listener asked, "Did they get the rabbit?" he wouldn't know how to follow the main purpose of the story through to the end. Avoid all interesting digressions from the development of the theme.

Climax. As each scene moves forward in logical and rapid sequence, the highest point of the story is reached. This is called the climax or the clash of forces. At this apex the story can grow no more intense. The mystery is explained or the solution is given. Interest declines when the great purpose of the narrative is revealed. Avoid relating another minor peak after this highest point is reached. This would result in an anti-climax.

The folk tales retold in many languages for centuries, follow this sequence of events. Bible stories, too, are excellent models. The storyteller can profitably analyze the struc-

ture of the great masters of the short-story — Hawthorne,
Poe, Stevenson, and De Maupassant. Robert Louis Stevenson's Samoan friends called him "Tusitala," their "teller of
tales."

THE ENDING OF THE STORY

Stop at the top. Don't go beyond the ending. After the
high pinnacle of the climax, there is little left to tell. Often
as in O'Henry's stories, the climax and the ending are the
same. Close your story at once, but not abruptly. It is much
more desirable to have your listeners sighing for more than
wriggling in restlessness at a long, drawn-out ending.
Imagination will supply any details desired following the
end. Children's stories have the swiftest endings, except
that of the anecdote.

Round out the story. Bring your listeners back to where
they started. One girl in describing the hot furnace for
glass-blowing, left the boys and girls staring into the hot
flames. At least bring them outside to normal temperature!

Account for all the characters. Fulfill all promises. Even
though the ending may be a surprise, the listener should be
able to think back and see where he had been prepared for
the conclusion. The mind must be satisfied with the ending.

Weave the moral into the story. The temptation to
moralize is a strong one. It is better to express the moral in
the words of the character or even by a fitting text of Scrip-
ture in the Bible story, than to add a teaching point as an
aftermath. Whatever application you wish to stress must be
given with the same animation and tone of voice used in the
story, or attention will be lost. The well-told story leads the
listener to think within himself: "He was so wicked, he
should be punished," or "If he could overcome that fault,
I know I can."

Most children agree with the little boy who said, "Never
mind the moral, give us another nanny goat," meaning
anecdote. Even a didactic point is lost when attention is
diverted.

Study story endings for models of completion. The folk
tales achieved their goals by adding, "They married and
lived happily ever after." Peter Asbjörnsen ended his Norse

tale of "The Three Billy-Goats Gruff" with a personal coup-
let after the goats were satisfied:

There the Billy-Goats got so fat they were scarcely able to
walk home again; and if the fat hasn't fallen off them, why
they're still fat; and so —

"Snip, snap, snout,
This tale's told out."

Howard Pyle in "The Apple of Contentment" asks the
listener to think through the moral for himself:

Now, that is all of this story. What does it mean? Can you
not see? Prut! Rub your spectacles and look again.

Examine these endings for swiftness and completeness:

Never after that did King Midas care for any gold except the
gold of the sunshine, and the gold of little Marygold's hair.
"The Golden Touch" — *Hawthorne*

* * *

Why, my necklace was paste. It was worth at most five
hundred francs!
"The Necklace" — *Guy De Maupassant*

* * *

And God saw everything that he had made, and, behold, it
was very good. And the evening and the morning were the
sixth day.

* * *

So David went his way, and Saul returned to his place.

* * *

And they went out of the prison, and entered into the house
of Lydia: and when they had seen the brethren, they comforted them, and departed.

* * *

DISCUSSION SUGGESTIONS

1. Why do we find the same fundamental stories in many
   different lands?
2. What is the secret of the universal appeal of the story?
3. In what respect are all stories alike?
4. What is the difference between a story for children and one
   for adults?
5. How does a story differ from a tale? A novel? A parable?
6. Why is the beginning of the story of such importance?
7. Should a child's story always end happily?
8. Where does the conflict enter into the story?
9. What are the necessary and the unnecessary incidents in a
   story?
10. What is the relationship of the title to the story?

STIMULATING READING

Moore, Annie. *Literature Old and New for Children*. New York:
Houghton Mifflin Co., 1934.
IV. "Folk Tales"
Esenwein, J. Berg. *Writing the Short Story*. New York: Noble
and Noble, Publishers, 1928.
IV of Part III. "A Laboratory Study of 'The Necklace,'" p. 324.

SUGGESTED PROJECTS

1. Show how a fairy story and how a Bible story each illustrate
   the principles of good structure.
2. Collect five good beginnings and five good endings of stories.
   Analyze them.
3. Analyze a story of Hawthorne, Poe, Stevenson, O'Henry, or
   some other great writer of the short-story.
4. Study the beginning and ending of a story in Part II.
5. Prepare an introduction for an Old and for a New Testament story.

CHAPTER V

HOW TO PREPARE A STORY

Burrow awhile and build broad on the roots of things.
— ROBERT BROWNING

"Storytelling is fun!" insisted Mrs. Ethel Barrett, popular radio and TV storytelling artist, "but you must be willing to work at the art! Allow an hour's preparation for every minute's production. The results are worth the effort!" Marie Shedlock practiced this same personal discipline when she taught, "The capacity for hard work, and even drudgery, is among the essentials of storytelling." All great art conceals art. When a story seems to flow with ease from the teller, be assured that the storyteller has made a friend of his story; he has saturated himself with it until it has become a part of his very nature.

Realizing how much a story influences the character of the listener, the storyteller makes thorough preparation. Children are quick to sense poor craftsmanship. The more the story is read and reread for its message, beauty, and striking discourse, the greater the sympathy and the possession of the story. "Every man is bound to leave a story better than he found it," wrote Mary A. Ward.

The previous chapters have stressed the general approach to all stories. This chapter explains the particular preparation for a specific story — its intensive analysis, and its condensing or enlarging. Dr. Walter L. Hervey sums up the points on the retelling of a story as:

> See it.
> Feel it.
> Shorten it.
> Expand it.
> Master it.
> Repeat it.

THE ANALYSIS OF THE STORY

State the central theme. This is the universal truth, the lesson, or the main point to be brought out in the story. It is like the bull's eye of the target; unless it is hit, the story just rambles along. Since art is indirect, we do not tell the listeners that they are all to be more kind after hearing this story, but we do strive to build up such a conception of kindness that the listener will think, "I want to be like that!" The teller will miss the whole point of the story if he fails to analyze his purpose in telling that particular story. The theme is like the soul of the narrative, and the plot its body.

The fairy tale of "Cinderella" portrays how humility is rewarded and pride punished. "The King of the Golden River" shows the power of love versus cruelty. The Bible story of "The Feeding of the Five Thousand" exemplifies so much more than just the consecration of the little lad or the great miracle Christ performed. It emphasizes both — teaching that little is multiplied in God's hand.

Locate the central theme, then build your story around that truth. Unity and harmony are laws of all the arts. In the Lille Museum hangs Millet's painting, "Feeding Her Birds." We are told that as Millet sat in his studio pondering a fit subject for his canvass, he looked out of his window and saw his wife feeding their three little children. What could be a more beautiful composition? Quickly he brushed with great strokes. But the picture seemed incomplete. Didn't he paint that his children might be fed? So around the corner of the house he sketched himself digging in the garden. Now every detail suggested the provision of both parents. As in art, the storyteller weaves each incident around the main theme.

Sense the mood or atmosphere of the story — its temper or spirit. What emotion is predominant? A patriotic story may be as stirring as a march tempo. The Biblical account of the fall of Jericho teems with excitement and triumph. The Christmas story of the Angel and the Shepherds demands the opposite in tone and manner — the hush of wonder and anticipation. The mood of the fairy tale is not the same as

Diagram of the Plot Development
of "The Shining Secret"

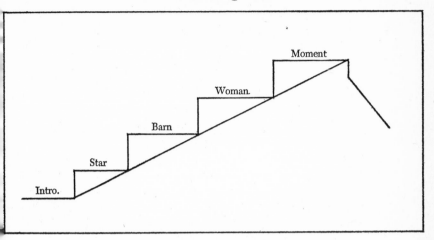

VALUE OF SUSPENSE

Suspense built by making each successive incident leading to the climax more arresting and vital.

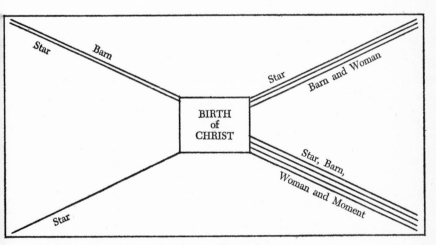

VALUE OF CHARACTERS

Incremental progression through additional characters, showing their relative value to the story.

CHART II

that of a biographical story. By tone and action create the desired atmosphere.

Know the characters. Steep yourself in their motives, individual traits, and conduct. How do they dress, speak, act? How old are they? What is their background and environment? Note their conversation. Do they speak in dialect, short sentences, or in an apologetic manner? Are they lovable, clever, despicable, or noble? If they could come to life and walk through your hall, would you recognize them? Children like direct discourse and actual conversations better than indirect statements. "I will," is more vivid than "She said that she would." Dickens once gave this advice to a young novelist: "Don't say, 'The woman screamed!' Bring her in and have her scream."

Build the scenes and incidents leading to the climax. This includes mastering the structure of the story — the beginning, pattern of sequence of events, and the ending. By picturing the episodes progressively, most of the "I forgot's" can be eliminated. Let each act lead as naturally to the next high point as the sure strokes of an artist. Study the necessary links in the chain of events. If you can cover two or three steps in one stride, do, but preserve the central impression. Weave this truth like a scarlet thread throughout the story as you progress. Action and suspense keep minds on tiptoe till the end. Capitalize on the highest point of the story.

It is helpful to diagram the progressive plot development of the story. Chart II (page 57) suggests an analysis of the story, "The Shining Secret," reprinted in Part II. This particular story builds each incident toward the climax, reaching it through incremental progression, by adding another detail at each upward step to the highest peak.

Note the language used. Read the story aloud to get the feel and flavor of the peculiar vocabulary and word pictures. The artist storyteller develops a sensitivity to words. There is a different cadence and diction for an Irish tale than for the Biblical narrative. Since the storyteller can not go far with a meager vocabulary, study synonyms and antonyms.

Train the ear to hear rhythmic phrases as the "drip, drip," of the rain on the porch, or the "trip, trap" of Billy-Goat

Gruff across the bridge. Sound words as "switch," "plop," and "crack" delight a child. The vowels and the "l," "m," "n," and "ng" consonant sounds are musical to the ear, while "s," "p," "t," "k," and "z" arouse to action. Fit the diction to the spirit of the story. Creative, image-making words are better than parrot-like, mechanical, or memorized words. Imagine the sounds, tastes, scents, and colors as though you were seeing and experiencing them. Past tense as "She saw," not "sees," is used in relating the story, but the present tense is reserved for all conversation.

For children, it may be necessary to recast the story in simple language. Use shorter sentences. "Simplify but do not sillify." Baffling words may be explained by paraphrasing them casually — "a damsel, a young girl, came to the door." Use unfamiliar words sparingly, then only when the context clarifies the meaning. Avoid equivocal words or those of double meaning.

Those who are tempted to use words beyond the vocabulary of the age group may check the word lists according to grades in such a book as Thorndike and Lorge.[1]

Vary transitional phrases rather than overworking "and," "next," or "again." "What do you suppose happened next?" or "You'll never guess what he saw," will keep interest progressing from point to point. In classical or Bible stories preserve the "whereupon's" and "wherefore's." How could the truth be more beautifully stated than "Where thou goest," or "Glory to God in the highest"? You may wish to memorize catchy refrains as the jingle repeated by Rumpelstiltsken or a Scriptural quotation. Be true to the expression of the author.

Such a careful analysis will help you to know your story. You will have "taken possession" of it until it partakes of the nature of a personal experience. Then you will delight to "produce" it for your listeners. "Take it," said Ruth Sawyer's Irish nurse, Johanna, "and may the next one who tells it, better it." Beth Caples applies this method of preparation:

[1]E. L. Thorndike and Irving Lorge, *The Teachers Word Book of 30,000 Words* (New York: Bureau of Publications, Teachers College, Columbia University, 1944).

After I have chosen the stories I begin to learn them by reading them over every day for a week at least. Then I outline them to see if I have the framework of the plot in mind. Then I test myself by trying to tell them from my outline to see where I need to refresh my memory. When I have the skeleton of the story well in mind, I tell it in my own words with all the zest and enjoyment I can bring to the telling. Never try to memorize the story unless it is an Andersen or a Kipling or an Oscar Wilde — where the style is so beautiful that the story loses all its flavor if not told in the original. But the old, familiar animal or folk tale should, I think, come through the teller's own personality. Share the fun and the suspense and the drama with the children as you tell the story.[2]

CONDENSING THE STORY

Many stories which we may profitably use, will need adapting before telling. Because of their length and often rambling structure, they may be cut without harming the original story. The silent reader depends on each descriptive detail. These ideas may be portrayed orally by tone of voice, a lift of the eyebrow, or a pause. While condensing the story, keep the theme in mind and look not aside from that purpose. Preserve the same viewpoint throughout, with a close, logical sequence.

Keep only the main characters. The younger the listener, the more confusing are too many names. Characters may be referred to by vocation as farmer or shepherd. They will be more easily remembered than by name. In the favorite stories of "The Three Pigs," "The Three Bears," and "The Three Billy-Goats Gruff," no proper names are mentioned but that of Goldilocks. Such phrases as "he said sternly," or "she hesitated before answering," may be omitted because the idea will be suggested in the manner of telling.

Eliminate all secondary threads of plot, selecting only those events which lead to the climax and are essential to that development. All details not consistent with the theme may be cut. Stories within a story are too complicated for children and are not needed for interest. Notice how Sara Cone Bryant condenses the story of "The King of the Golden

[2]Head of the Children's Department of the Enoch Pratt Free Library in Baltimore, Maryland. In a personal letter.

River" by eliminating many references to the incident of the West Wind.[3]

Choose descriptive details carefully. Some would leave out most of the description. While we may shorten this, we must beware of omitting the emotional elements of background often essential to the action of the story. Don't have the characters acting on an empty stage. A word or two inserted while telling the incident is better than several sentences of description together. Keep more than a skeleton of the story. Certain words are stereotypes in our thinking. We don't need to describe a policeman, butcher, fairy, or engineer since those concepts are already clear in our minds.

ENLARGING THE STORY

A few incidents are so dramatic that they will want to be enlarged to full story length. By gathering more facts and background and by imaginatively realizing the picture, we can heighten the effect of the story. Alice D. Miller has cleverly retold the story of "Cinderella" in poetic form. Well illustrated, its sparkling humor is enjoyed by adults as well as by children. Agnes Sligh Turnbull, in *Far Above Rubies*, has enlarged several of the stories of Bible women without harming the original account.

Avoid all unnecessary padding just for the sake of elaboration. Add only those details or incidents which are logical and true to the author's intent. Let the imagination picture reactions and scenes. In historical and Biblical incidents, preserve accuracy of costume, period, and choice of name. Search for details which reveal the nature of the main character. Visit the locality of the story or author, if possible.

Augusta Stevenson, famous for her series of *Childhood Stories of Famous Americans*, once told me how carefully she did research for each story. After completing the study for *Sitting Bull* concerning the Sioux Indians of South Dakota, she showed her manuscript to a contemporary Sioux whom she met in Florida. He complimented her upon her faithful portrayal of Indian life, both in facts and in conversational characteristics. She enlarged the historical

[3]*How to Tell Stories to Children* (New York: Houghton Mifflin Co., 1933), p. 64.

incident by minor details which kept the action moving and preserved the spirit of the people.

I have found that interviews with interesting people and visits to historical places are a great source of inspiration and material in enlarging stories. While relating several such incidents in the life of John Wesley in my course in *Christian Biography,* an adult slipped into the back of the room during the story hour. Later she remarked, "I have read the life of Wesley, but I never heard some of those incidents. Where did you find them?" They are not found by reading one biography. Side references in history and literature often prove rewarding. The storyteller just keeps searching. Stories are not built overnight. Be sure of the facts before using incidents in true stories.

ANALYSIS OF THE PARABLE OF THE PRODIGAL SON

Charles Dickens, when asked to name the greatest short story written, answered, "The Parable of the Prodigal Son." From the viewpoint of structure alone, this parable of only five hundred words, with no proper names for characters, is a model of construction. Each word is carefully chosen with a direct bearing on the purpose of the whole.

The parables are unique in literature and religious teaching. Dr. Thornton Whaling once made an exhaustive study of the religious literature of all nations, but found no parallels to the parables in the New Testament.[4] When Daniel Webster was a young student, his biographer tells us, he disparaged the parables. His minister told him to write one of his own. He tried it, then decided that no human teacher could do it. "Never man spake like this man."

Turn to Luke 15:11-32. The first words, "A certain man," tell us at once that this is a story of character. If it had begun, "A long time ago in the land of Judea," et cetera, the setting, not the character, would have been predominant. These words also reveal that the father, not the prodigal, is the main character. Perhaps the title of this parable is misleading. Then the two sons, and the younger are mentioned in order of importance.

[4]Robert C. McQuilkin, "Knowing the Parables — Miracles of Teaching," *Sunday School Times,* (January 28, 1933), Vol. 75, No. 4, p. 64.

What is the central theme? We read a story of a son who ran away from home, but returned and was forgiven; of an older brother who remained with his father, but lost the spirit of service. Many, many lessons may be drawn from this parable, but only one truth is outstanding, illustrated by these incidents — the love and forgiveness of the father. This is paramount. This is the point of emphasis to be kept in both the original story and the spiritual allegory.

Note the conflicts from the very first verse — the dissatisfaction of the younger son, his demand for his share of the inheritance, the far country, the wasted living, the poverty of body and soul. When "he came to himself" and said, "I will arise . . . ," we see the subjective climax in this character which foretells the outcome of the story. The objective climax is reached when his father welcomes him home.

But why have two sons? Wouldn't the father's great compassion be realized in the forgiveness of the younger son? How does the addition of an elder son enhance this truth? An only son might be more readily forgiven for he must carry on the family name. A younger son could be turned away since he had a brother to carry on the inheritance. Hence, the father's forgiveness is even more magnanimous. When the lost is found both physically and spiritually, we are satisfied. Thus, in structure alone, we find a complete, well-developed story.

Since about ninety per cent of Biblical language is composed of Anglo-Saxon words of one or two syllables, the pictures are already vivid. Phrases such as "far country," "came to himself," "no more worthy," "fatted calf," "safe and sound," are a part of our literary heritage. Preserve their beauty and cadence in the telling.

While we condemn the younger son for leaving his father's house, we will want to tell the story sympathetically, trusting that he will repent and return home. Catch the mood of rejoicing when the prodigal is forgiven and restored.

DISCUSSION SUGGESTIONS

1. Why should the storyteller analyze his story so thoroughly?
2. Explain the terms: theme, mood, and climax.
3. When might it be wise to adapt a story?

4. What is the difference between a story adapted and one retold?
5. How does an oral story differ from a printed one in diction?
6. Where would you look for background material for the atmosphere of stories of King Arthur? Uncle Remus? the Bible?
7. How can you fit your vocabulary to the story?
8. Why is it advisable to use direct discourse in stories?

STIMULATING READING

BRYANT, SARA CONE. *How to Tell Stories to Children.* New York: Houghton Mifflin Co., 1933.

"The Red Thread of Courage," p. 76-81 (enlarged story)

MILLER, ALICE D. *Cinderella.* Coward-McCann, Inc., 1943. (enlarged story)

TURNBULL, AGNES SLIGH. *The Maid of Emmaus,* in Part II. (condensed from original enlargement)

SUGGESTED PROJECTS

1. Compare the stories listed above with their originals.
2. Using the different sense appeals, describe a summer night, the approach of a train, a church, a multitude, and the home of Mary and Martha.
3. Analyze five stories from Part II for theme, mood, characters, incidents, climax, and language.
4. Condense the story of Ruth from the Old Testament book.
5. Adapt a story from a classical source.
6. Elaborate on the Biblical account of the little lame prince recorded in II Samuel 4: 4 and 9: 1-13.
7. Enlarge an anecdote or a fable.

Chapter VI

HOW TO TELL A STORY

He ceas'd, but left so pleasing on the ear, his voice, that listening still they seemed to hear.

— HOMER

Henry Ward Beecher was once asked what he would do if a member of his audience went to sleep while he was preaching. "I'd ask the janitor to get a long pole, put a sharp prod on the end of it, and tell him," he explained, "to prod the preacher!"

Gaining attention and holding interest is the responsibility of the storyteller. Thorough preparation makes the story a real experience that you want to share. When the hungry expression on a little face is erased, and the mischievous lad listens in rapt enjoyment, you will receive the reward for all your detailed study. A student of mine, after telling her first story in the classroom as a teacher, sensed this when she said, "It was so quiet that I was scared!"

ATTITUDE

Avoid a professional manner. Much of the storyteller's success depends upon her sincerity and naturalness. Keep a childlike appreciation; be a child of yesterday.

Be wholehearted and enthusiastic. Don't tell things without making them real. Emerson taught that "Nothing great was ever achieved without enthusiasm." Impression precedes expression — this is ever the secret of art. When you are intimate with the characters and the sequence of events and catch the spirit of the narrative, storytelling will become the spontaneous outpouring of this experience. A love of the beautiful and the true, and a love of people results in an enriched personality. Your own animation and buoyant feeling will so empathize your listeners that they will catch

65

a little of your own wholeheartedness. "Always trying out with others something that had moved me deeply; always finding out that what had been for me a spiritual feast usually fed others," wrote Ruth Sawyer.

Be friendly and earnest. You may be funny but not flip. Though weighed down with the solemness of your message, be pleasant. A genuine, unaffected, warm smile and a confident, poised manner, do much to hold attention. Dovie Yeatts Insall, editor of *Story Art Magazine,* expresses a deeper truth when she writes:

> The storyteller needs *Love of God.* For if one has love of God in one's heart it will follow that he will also have love of his fellow man. For without love we become as "sounding brass or tinkling symbols."[1]

Another member of the National Story League, adds:

> It is close communion with God: — the silent prayer the second before facing an audience; and, after the last spoken word, — the silent prayer of every storyteller, "Thank Thee, God, — for your gift to me of Storytelling."[2]

Shun a line-by-line memorization which gives a stilted delivery. Learn your story orally with book in hand, sitting or standing before an imaginary audience. Tell it aloud once or twice. Read special portions for the particular cadence and the folk flavor. Absorb it by assimilation. Live with your characters. Brood over your story; recreate it imaginatively. Tell it to the darkness after you've gone to bed, or think it out on the bus. Learn it with the heart. Visualize an old castle and Sleeping Beauty or Ruth gleaning in the fields, not a printed page.

Regardless of your method, it is well to memorize a rhythmic refrain or an applicable quote which may give the distinctive flavor of the story. Marie Shedlock considered both learning by heart and telling in her own words necessary to an all-around storyteller. The method depends on the kind of story. "If the style is classic, or if the interest of the story is closely connected with the style, as in Andersen's,

---

[1] "A Storyteller Needs—," *Story Art Magazine,* November-December, 1957, p. 5. Used with permission.
[2] Ruth Ragsdale, "The Storytelling Key" Ibid., p. 11. Used with permission.

Kipling's, or Stevenson's, then it is better to commit it absolutely to memory."[3]

PHYSICAL ARRANGEMENT

The storyteller must create the mood and the atmosphere for the listeners. He depends upon it. As George Herbert found, "No tale so good but may be spoiled in the telling."

The time of day will affect the response. Children respond differently at an opening assembly than after recess or at bedtime. Sunset is an ideal time at a summer camp. At this appropriate hour at the University of Wisconsin, we looked forward to the stories of the naturalist, John Muir, told weekly by the Curator of the Museum on the beach of Lake Mendota. Consider the hour.

The order and attractiveness of the room itself may increase attention. An overflowing wastebasket or cluttered shelves are bound to distract. Is the temperature comfortable, the atmosphere happy? In one of his public lectures, Dr. Clyde M. Narramore, Consulting Psychologist of Los Angeles County Schools, told how he used sacred records to stimulate stories for his four-year-old daughter. After the bedtime prayer, the playing of *The Old Rugged Cross* encouraged her to ask, "What is the cross, Daddy?" Then he told her the story of love.

The seating should be comfortable. You may group your listeners around you on rugs or on the grass, arranged in a semi-circle. This is more informal than the row by row seating of the classroom. Be sure each one listening can see the storyteller with a direct eye-contact. Keep the smaller ones in front. Seat them so that their backs are to any late-arrivals.

The smaller the group, the more individual and effective the response. Try to divide your listeners into groups under thirty. The large groups depend on mass response and demand a more formal presentation, as from a platform in an auditorium. It is a great help to know the names of the children. One camp director I know, studies the enrollment sheets and learns the names and personal information of each camper before the opening day. This gives a great advantage to the storyteller.

The storyteller in the center of the semicircle or directly opposite, may sit or stand as she chooses, depending on her eyehold and the number listening. She may feel happier to sit when her audience is smaller in both size and age. However, with a group of twenty-five wigglers from three to seven years, I usually stood or walked or moved. Then the group sat still on their own little red chairs!

BODILY ACTION

Empathy is the unconscious muscular reaction to that which we see — an inner mimicry. Children look and act at the suggestion of the storyteller. His actions may emphasize them positively so they are relaxed, eager, and attentive. On the other hand, he may negatively empathize them by a nervous, uncontrolled manner making them troublesome and restless. A forgetfulness of self and a possession of the message will result in poise and attention. Self-confidence is gained by preparation and practice.

Posture should be natural, not stilted. Sit tall, stand tall, and think tall. Avoid sitting or standing sloppily. Keep hands free of pencils, handkerchief, dress buttons, or any other unconscious mannerism. Self-consciousness may be betrayed by a nervous twisting of the handkerchief — a fault felt but not defined. Forget yourself.

Directness is most important. By looking directly at your listeners in a friendly manner, you may gauge your effectiveness. Heads bent over quarterlies or notes lose valuable contact. A direct eye-hold creates a "just-between-ourselves" atmosphere — a friendliness reaching out to share. Coleridge describes this response of the wedding guest to the Ancient Mariner's tale:

> He holds him with his glittering eye;
>   The Wedding Guest stood still,
> And listens like a three years' child —
>   The Mariner hath his will.

Keep listeners interested in the "what" of your story, not the "how" of your telling. Why break into your story with rebukes for squirming? If Johnny and his friends in the back row are restless, weave their names into the story to catch their interest anew. "You three boys in the back row could never guess" will challenge more attention than direct reprimands.

Gestures want to be brief and suggestive, not studied. An imitative gesture indicating the size of Midas' pile of gold will enhance the story rather than detract from it. With smaller audiences, a movement of the finger or twinkle of the eye will be sufficient to suggest your meaning. The subtle expression of the face, the glance of the eyes, nod of the head, warning frown, shrug of the shoulders — all help to create the mental image and changing mood desired.

Movement when related to the story will help to carry the meaning. Children learn by imitation. The younger the group, the more visible the bodily action required. In a large auditorium, people hear best with their eyes, so enlarge the scope of your action. Telling a story to hundreds of children calls for a platform technique. In such a situation, Marie Shedlock became the dramatic reader. Bill Martin, facing all the elementary children from three of the city schools, used a microphone and asked for participation in the telling of his well-loved, "The Brave Little Indian." Cliff Barrows, of the Billy Graham team, necessarily uses elaborate pantomine to illustrate his Bible stories for the thousands of children in his audiences. With 12,000 children in his Portland rally, it is no wonder he was called the "Pied Piper of Evangelism." He says regarding his method:

> The story itself is told as simply as possible and yet with as much illustration as far as acting is concerned as I am able to do to try to help make the story live. It would be a little bit different if you were in a church building or some smaller auditorium with a smaller number of kiddies. But when you have large auditoriums or arenas and are many, many feet away from the kiddies up in the balcony, it is hard to hold their attention unless you move around and do things a little out of the ordinary and that is what we have tried to do and still make the story as effective as possible.[4]

On the other hand, Gudrun Thorne-Thomsen, facing smaller groups, held complete attention with hardly a move of her finger. Do not over-dramatize. The storyteller is not

[4]From personal letter.

playing the part of the story. He seeks to arouse the imagination of the hearers to picture the scene for themselves. The storyteller is ever the observer, the reporter, the interpreter. A good principle to observe is: Never let your action draw attention to itself or it becomes faulty.

Characters may be identified by indicating position and by change of tone. Avoid turning the head in the same direction for all dialogue. Height of glance and direction help to separate characters.

Mary Gould Davis taught:

> It is not until we know a story thoroughly and feel it deeply that we are free to interpret it. This freedom, when a story is completely ours, is physical as well as mental. It brings us a definite sense of physical power. It sweeps away the flat, monotonous voice, the tense body, the self-conscious expression. The high head-notes that are always a sign of self-consciousness deepen to the fresh, full tones that come from throat and chest. Our gestures become logical and graceful because we do not deliberately make gestures![5]

VOICE

The storyteller's voice may have the subtle charm of a musical instrument in creating imagination and in holding attention, or it may irritate causing restlessness and indifference. The super-sweetened voice which talks down to the "dee-ah lit-tle chil-dren," will hinder, not help. Natural, sincere, warm, and friendly tones draw the listeners to the storyteller.

The *quality* of the voice reveals personality to such a degree that a child quickly recognizes sincerity. Good storytellers suggest a different tone for each new idea — warmth for love, strength for courage, and sad, strained tones for hunger. Tones portray truer feelings than the words themselves.

A few moments of daily practice will enable you to improve your speech techniques. Any good speech text will contain exercises so necessary for proper diaphragmatic breathing, relaxation, and resonance. Make a recording of your voice. Ask your classmates and instructor to note any

[5] *Once Upon a Time*, pamphlet prepared by the New York Library Association, p. 8. Used with permission.

tendency to monotony, harshness, or wasted breath. Face your faults honestly and strive for a pleasing quality and effective expression. Interpretation may be greatly increased by reading poetry, especially the Psalms, aloud daily. Keep your voice in tune.

Shakespeare emphasized the pleasant quality of voice when he wrote of Cordelia in *King Lear:*

> Her voice was ever soft,
> Gentle, and low, an excellent thing in woman.

Rate or timing may make the difference between a mediocre and a magnetic voice in storytelling. Some stories amble along to a standstill, others march with a brisk "left-right," or gallop with the "tlot-tlot" of the horse. The gentle fall of the rain that increased in rate and force to a downpour and flood during the time of Noah, may be portrayed through vocal timing. To preserve the varied rhythm of conversation, speak important phrases more slowly. Action requires a more rapid rate. When the prodigal son returned to his father and made his confession, his father interrupted with his command to bring forth the best robe. Many hesitate between these two verses, thus implying that the father was slow to forgive his son.

Pause, if effective, heightens suspense. "The king looked into the furnace and saw . . ." Hold the idea so that each listener will ask himself, "Saw what?" Capitalize on the high peaks of a story. "He opened the door, and there stood — — the princess." Often a child will give the right answer aloud in his absorbed attention, but his response never disturbs the story. A pause "pulls up" the attention of the listeners and challenges them to think through the outcome.

Dr. Daniel Poling once told us at a convention of his experience while telling tiny tots the story of Baby Moses. When he had finished he asked, "Do you have any questions?" One child raised her hand and asked, "What makes your mouth go so fast when you talk?"

Change of pitch is basic for storytelling. Too high-pitched a voice not only strains the teller, but also tenses the hearers, resulting in restlessness. Both will enjoy the story hour more fully if the voice is pitched properly. Avoid monotony by varying the inflections so suggestive of subtle meanings not caught in silent reading. Upward inflections keep the listeners attentive; downward inflections suggest finality.

Volume must be sufficient to be heard easily by all without strain. When building up a climax, increase the volume, raise the pitch, and decrease the rate. Don't try to talk above noise, but lower the voice demanding attention. Even though you are separated by only a screen from another class, you may have effective emphasis and feeling.

Articulation should be clear. Since children imitate what they hear, a good storyteller is careful of his pronunciation and enunciation. He avoids slovenly speech and the dropping of his final consonants. The vowels add beauty of tone; the consonants, understanding. The child who illustrated the manger scene after hearing "Silent Night," added a fat, jolly man. When asked to identify him, he explained, "That's 'round John Virgin.'" His mind had not comprehended "round yon virgin."

Use various qualities of voice to fit your characters — from the deep rumble of the giant to the sweet falsetto of the fairies. While we never impersonate the voice of God, we do quote His words with dignity, calmness, and compassion. Practice interrupting yourself if you would portray natural dialogue. In this sound-conscious age, we use many onomatopoeias suggestive of the choo-choo of the train, the roar and pop of flames, or the sputter of the truck's engine.

Ireene Wicker, radio story artist, was adept in portraying the personality of her characters by tone. As with our bodily action, all these additions must be closely knit to the story, and not become just decorative attachments. The Chinese have a proverb: "When the words cease, the meaning flows on."

> Start low,
> Proceed slow,
> Rise higher
> Take fire
> When most impressed
> Be self-possessed;
> To spirit wed form;
> Sit down in a storm!

THE FOLLOW-UP

Marie Shedlock recommended five minutes of silence following the telling of the story. To bring an exalted listener immediately to earth is like having a slap in the face. The mood so carefully created must be preserved. Don't ruin the story by questions to test knowledge or by asking for a retelling at once.

Children are often dismissed after a story hour. They fall asleep at bedtime. But in the classroom there are several wise, creative activities for a follow-up. Let each sit at his desk or go to the blackboard to illustrate the story he has heard. Boys and girls are keen observers and often draw details accurately. Do not expect art work.

It is very natural for the children on their own initiative to want to act out the story, especially on the playground. I recall one girl who rewrote one of Poe's stories in poetry. Some like to make puppets. A retelling of the story by the child the next day will expose any false impressions and will help him to develop good voice and vocabulary for himself. Clay modeling, booklets to illustrate, and appropriate games, are all a part of the creative activities associated with the story hour.

EVALUATION CHART

The storyteller may test his own delivery by asking classmates or adult listeners to evaluate his telling on the five-point score sheet suggested. (See Chart III.) Review the importance of each point carefully. Keep a record of your own progress. When the rules are mastered, abandon yourself to the joy of your story.

DISCUSSION SUGGESTIONS

1. How do the seating and room arrangements aid in storytelling?
2. Show how the attitude of the storyteller affects the listener.
3. What are the disadvantages of memorizing a story verbatim? What are the advantages?
4. How may you overcome any self-consciousness?
5. Why do you prefer to sit or stand when telling a story?
6. How much bodily action should a storyteller have?
7. How does the voice affect the listeners?

Story-Telling Score Sheet

STORY-TELLING SCORE SHEET	INTERPRE-TATION Appreciation Imagination Sympathy Mood	VOICE Tone Quality Articulation Flexibility Volume	ACTION Animation Posture Gesture Character-ization	STRUCTURE Sequence of events Descriptions Language Climax	GENERAL EFFECT Empathy Poise Audience Stimulation	TOTAL SCORE
NAME	20	20	20	20	20	100·

CHART III

8. What is the importance of the pause?
9. Why is a direct "eye-hold" essential?
10. Whose responsibility is it when a story fails to interest the listener?

STIMULATING READING

SORRENSON, FRED. *Speech for the Teacher.* New York: Ronald
    Press Co., 1952.
      III. "Bodily Action"
      V, VI. "Voice"
SHEDLOCK, MARIE. *The Art of the Storyteller.*
      III. "The Artifices of Story-Telling"
SAWYER, RUTH. *The Way of the Storyteller.*
      VIII. "A Technique to Abolish Technique"

SUGGESTED PROJECTS

1. Criticize a recording of your own voice.
2. Practice voice exercises for breathing, resonance, and relaxation.
3. Practice tongue twisters and exercises for flexibility of the articulators.
4. Listen critically to a radio story. Note how the characters are distinguished.
5. Suggest the voice of each in this familiar story: "It's I, the (littlest, the middle-sized, the biggest) Billy-Goat Gruff coming over your bridge."
6. Practice the syllable "oh" in ten different mood situations such as surprise, regret, delight, etc.
7. Choose a fable or a short dialogue passage from Part II, and practice interrupting yourself and the characters.
8. Tell a significant incident that occurred in the life of a great artist, scientist, or missionary.

CHAPTER VII

HOW TO USE BIBLE STORIES

Without a parable, spake He not unto them.
— MATTHEW 13:34

"When I returned from shopping," a mother told me, "I found pencil marks on the freshly painted white woodwork. Both of my little children, when asked, denied having done it. I said nothing at the time. A little later, my boy, about four years old, was so quiet that I investigated. Going into the next room, I saw him standing in the corner, mumbling something to himself over and over. As I listened, I heard him repeating the verse we had learned in connection with the Bible story that week, 'Be sure your sin will find you out. Be sure your sin will find you out.'"

Bible stories develop a spiritual awareness. They are the rich, moral heritage of every child. When working closely with children, it is possible to find just that Bible story which supplements their experiences and reveals the answer to a problem. The Scriptures are the greatest source of character-building stories. Incidents from the lives of the Bible heroes help to develop courage, decision, unselfishness, and purpose. No better story of friendship is known than that of David and Jonathan; of a daughter-in-law, than that of Ruth and Naomi; of a true neighbor, than that of the Good Samaritan.

William Thompson, known as "Bendigo," was once champion pugilist of England. But at sixty, he occupied a prison cell for the twenty-seventh time. He paid no attention to the chapel services until one time the account of the contest between David and Goliath was read. He followed the reading so intently that he forgot where he was, and shouted, "Bravo! Bravo! I'm glad the little 'un won!" After he returned to his cell, he paced back and forth considering

76

how unequally matched the men were. He came to the conclusion that God must have helped the little one. He became interested in reading the Scriptures, and in time was saved to live a victorious life.

Angelo Patri, authority and counselor on children, a regular contributor to the Boston *Herald,* wrote in his column:

> More than once a month the question comes, "What book can I give my child that will help him to form a fine character, to understand the real values of life? I'd like one that gave him a fine cultural background, too." To all such searchers I have one book to offer — a fountain of wisdom and inspiration all his days — the Bible.

Every type of story is found in the Bible. Classical literature ignores children, but the Bible is full of references to them. There are the wonder stories more appealing than fairy tales. There is the great Hebrew epic rich in the lives of the patriarchs. Add to these the stirring drama of Job, and the biographical, historical, and romantic stories of both the Old and New Testaments. Katherine Cather, educator and storyteller, emphatically says:

> If one knows the Bible well enough, it is possible from it alone to satisfy every story need of the child from infancy to manhood. But this can be done only by those to whom the life and thought of the Hebrews is as familiar as the narratives themselves.[1]

Every age delights in well-told Bible stories. They are excellent models. Saturated with human interest, they satisfy the intellectual, aesthetic, and moral senses. They become a medium of culture, a standard of ethics, and a builder of ideals for everyone. They abound in color, adventure, imagery, and action.

An elementary public schoolteacher told me that she kept Bible story books with others on a table in the back of the room. When a pupil had finished his work, he could choose which book he wished to read. The Bible story books wore out first, she observed. In our community, an elderly lady successfully presents a Bible story with the aid of felt flannelgraph figures in various adult clubs. Radio and TV

[1] *Religious Education through Storytelling* (Cincinnati: The Abingdon Press, 1925), p. 176.

producers and professional storytellers have long been aware of the attraction of the Bible story to all ages.

In recalling the looked-forward-to daily periods when her mother not only told, but read aloud the Bible stories, Ruth Sawyer writes of the need of such a continued practice in this century:

> To think that children of today, faced with the world of tomorrow, might be experiencing this daily fellowship with that book which, above all others, can strengthen faith in God and mankind. We need this strengthening if ever peace is to endure, if we are to have world unity.[2]

Every principle used in the preparation of other stories is applicable to Bible stories, plus (1) an attitude of reverence, (2) a knowledge of the background, and (3) the adaptation of sources from the whole Bible. In addition to the standards of good storytelling already established, we would emphasize these particular approaches.

ATTITUDE

Preserve the sense of reality. Unless you approach the Bible stories with an attitude of belief and respect, it will be difficult to tell them. Let the truth grip you before you expect your listeners to grasp it. Plan and pray over your presentation that the spirit of the story may be preserved and caught. Bible stories are truth and must be distinguished from the folk tales which teach a lesson and are often patterned after them. However, we must avoid assuming a special, sacred manner. Bible characters are real flesh-and-blood people who rise and fall, fail and succeed, as we.

One much-loved teller of Bible stories always begins with a travelogue, tracing the route to Palestine by train, ship, or plane, establishing a greater credence to the account. He never refers to the Bible as, "It says," but quotes the writer or the book. By holding, or having near, an open Bible, the reality of the story is realized more graphically by the listeners.

Present the fundamental truths with simplicity. The basic teachings of life, the creation, the birth of Christ, His crucifixion and resurrection, are not hard to present when told

[2] "On Reading the Bible Aloud," *Horn Book* (March-April, 1945), Vol. XXI, No. 2, p. 99. Used with permission.

in the language of the Scriptures. What the Bible says is greater than the opinion or creed of the teller. The age group will determine the details of moral teaching. To youngsters it is not necessary to explain why Joseph was put into prison. The little boy who prayed to be like Jesus when He was six, caught the significance of the moral truth.

BACKGROUND

Study the historical and geographical background in detail. Fortunately there has been excellent research on the customs, dress, and even the weather conditions in Palestine. All these details add interest and accuracy. Unless these facts are known, the children will wonder why the shepherds were not cold sleeping outdoors at our Christmas time. How were houses constructed so that the men who brought the paralytic to Jesus could open up the roof? Why should a lily be compared to Solomon and royalty and not to a bride? We think of lilies as white, but Eastern field lilies were scarlet in color. Know the facts and be true to them.

Lord Kitchener knew his geography of the Holy Land so well from his mother's Bible stories, that when Lord George sent him to Palestine to survey during World War I, he could recognize most of the localities. General Lew Wallace was able to clearly and accurately picture the seting for *Ben Hur* without visiting the Holy Land. The secret of his descriptive ability was the meticulous care with which he planned and organized his task. He drew topographical maps of the country. By plotting the streets, squares, walls, temples, and buildings of Jerusalem, and by sketching the floor plans of the Jewish and Roman houses in which his characters lived, he thoroughly prepared himself to write.

Trace the various parallel passages. Read the story first from the King James' version noted for its beauty of diction and structure. Study other passages to throw light on your particular story. Use a good Harmony of the Gospels for New Testament incidents. There are many references to the Old Testament characters in the New. To the Exodus account of Moses, for instance, add the further details found in *Hebrews* and in *Revelation*. We often stress his refusal to be a son of a temporal Pharaoh, but by-pass his eternal reward as a son of the King of kings with multitudes singing the song of Moses and the Lamb. Note that the story of the "Feeding of the Five Thousand" took place near Passover time. By this we would know that it was springtime. Springtime means green hills, fair weather, et cetera. The text speaks of "grassy hillsides."

Other versions, commentaries, Bible story books, and lesson helps will aid you in saturating yourself with the living story. Keep a Bible dictionary, geography, and concordance handy during preparation. Colored photographs, charts, and illustrations are available and profitable in stimulating imagination.

Check pronunciation of Bible names. Proper nouns may be found in a self-pronouncing Bible or Bible Dictionary. Children like the music of names; they prefer "Shadrach, Meshach, and Abednego" to the "Three Hebrew Children." Little words, like "saith," "sword," "forehead," "apostle," and "deluge," are often mispronounced. Thorough preparation rewards both the storyteller and the listeners.

ADAPTATION

Analyze your theme. After the story has been properly studied and assimilated, you are free to make your own arrangement, keeping true to the spirit of the text. Your specific purpose will be the golden thread determining the choice of incidents throughout the whole story. In the story of the "Three Hebrew Children," their conviction or decision of purpose is honored. Ruth is rewarded for her "steadfastness." The friendship vow of David and Jonathan is expressed in David's care for Jonathan's son, Mephibosheth, years later. The story of the intercessory prayer of Abraham is often concluded without relating the answer which is recorded in later chapters.

Choose a single chain of events. Every episode will want to be progressive and vivid, not just something happening. Keep the action in relation to the character, and work toward a definite climax. Continued stories of Joseph, Paul, and Christ hold interest as incident after incident — each a complete story — are told. The more familiar the story, the more careful the preparation of an attention-getting beginning with atmosphere and conflict. One storyteller began the story of Stephen with the cry, "Stone him! Stone him!" then flashed back to the situation.

Keep the same point of view. Most Bible stories are told in third person as by an observer. However, you might gain greater interest by telling a well-known story from a different angle. Why not tell of the Baby Moses from the outlook of Miriam, the junior sister? For beginners, the story of Noah's Ark as if told by the dove, portrays a varied account, yet can be true to the Word. The story of the four men who brought the paralytic to Jesus would vary according to the teller: the paralytic himself, the disciples, the four friends, or the scribes.

I once prepared a series of junior lessons on the book of *The Acts* in the form of a radio broadcast. The headlines served to outline the story. Descriptions and explanation were easily woven into the account by the reporter as an eye-witness. This beginning following the station identification may serve as a suggestion:

Come in . . . Jerusalem . . .

Events are moving swiftly since the feast of Pentecost and the organization of the Church. A lame man leaps at the Beautiful Gate. Peter and John are arrested in the Temple. Elders try the Apostles. The Name of Jesus Christ is exalted. These are the headlines. Turn to Acts III and IV while I give you a detailed report . . .

A notable miracle has indeed taken place in this holy city. About three o'clock in the afternoon, your time, or the "ninth hour" of the day here, Peter, the apostle who preached that moving sermon, and John, the youngest of the twelve, were walking together toward the shining Temple for the hour of prayer. Entering the Royal Porch, they crossed the Court of the Gentiles, and came to the gate of the Temple which is called Beautiful. In the shade of a marble pillar a lame man sat on his haunches, stretching out his hollowed palms to beg alms. . . .

Preserve the beauty of language. Sara Cone Bryant urged the telling of Bible stories because they are "from a source unsurpassed in literature for purity of style and loftiness of content."[3] Nevertheless, many problems in diction will

[3]*How to Tell Stories to Children* (New York: Houghton Mifflin Co., 1933), p. 52.

arise. A substitution of the modern terms, "gangster" for "robbers," or "barbecue" for "fatted calf," gives an entirely different concept from the original. Words such as "mad," "guy," "crazy," "kids," or "daddy," detract from the purity and beauty of Bible language. Such words as "kine," or "damsel," not now used, may need to be altered, but the "wherefore" and "it came to pass," are typical Bible transitions. The storyteller who illustrated the strong man by naming Joe Louis rather than Samson, took imaginations far afield from the Bible atmosphere. The word "priest" has a different connotation today than when used in Bible times.

Children love repetition. Picture Naaman dipping into the river one, two, three, five, seven times, not all at once. The dialogue between God and Abraham grows in interest as you run down the numbers, "For the sake of 50, 45, 40, 30, 20, and 10 . . . I will spare the city." To call "Samuel, Samuel," three different times, is more intensely realized than to tell us indirectly that God called him three times.

Often the conversation can be couched in no better language than the original. Repeat those majestic lines again and again until the listener catches their euphony and rhythm. Any shepherd story is incomplete without Psalm 23. You may wish to include the reading of a specific passage with your story.

Translate Bible terms and measurements into today's comparison. An image threescore cubits high means little to a child. Ninety feet high is accurate, but "about the height of a flagpole" or "fifteen men six feet tall" creates a clearer mental picture. Study the distances of Palestine. How tall was Goliath? How heavy was his coat of mail? What was the size of the Ark, of the Temple?

Avoid leaving a false impression. One storyteller admired Daniel because he would eat no meat! It was meat offered to idols that was refused. The condemning of human sacrifices practiced in Canaan is a vital part of the story of Abraham offering Isaac. Preserve the glorious triumph of Christianity marching on through the ages.

In giving the story of Daniel in the lions' den, one teller told of the angel's shutting the lions' mouths. Later, when she described the lions eating up Daniel's persecutors, a child raised his hand, questioning, "But the lions couldn't eat them. Their mouths were closed!" Since children's imaginations are so realistic, these little explanations that adults take for granted must be clarified.

Round out the plot satisfactorily, keeping the application woven throughout the whole story. Often we close with a Bible quotation that clinches the truth. But listeners grow restless when a teller says, "So we must learn that . . ." The ideals upheld within the story are more impressive than those "tacked on." In the story of Ruth who forsook both her country and her gods, the climax is frequently lost in the telling. Not only did she marry Boaz, but she also became the grandmother of David through whom Christ was born. This incident is needed to complete the theme.

Should we add imaginary incidents or characters to a Bible story? Not if they give a wrong or different impression. Put nothing into the story by way of explanation which the Bible does not include in principle, whether in incident or character, which will have to be recalled or modified when the child grows older. It is not irreverent to suggest what some character might have said, providing the words fit him and the personality of the Bible heroes. We might "suppose" that Hannah made a little red coat for Samuel, though the color is not mentioned.

Martha S. Hooker, storyteller and child-evangelist, says regarding this point:

I believe that the Bible stories should be told accurately as far as the Bible text is concerned. Whenever an idea is introduced which might be implied but is not in the text, I think it well to add the words, "it might have been," or if referring to a house, for instance, the storyteller might add, "It might have been a white, flat-roofed house with steps leading up from the outside if like the houses of that day."[4]

Imagination based upon research regarding the background helps to picture many of these details. Name some of the different animals from elephant to snail which entered the ark. We know that all were represented. God created not only fish, but the little fishes, middle-sized fishes, and the big fishes. The sound effects of the "clump, clump" of

[4]From personal letter.

the donkey down the road, or of the silence after the clattering of the dishes and the babble of voices when the writing appeared on the wall, all aid in making the story lifelike.

> Fill the vessel to the brim;
> Leave the miracle to Him
> To turn the water into wine.

VISUAL AIDS

The question, "Should we use visual aids with the Bible story?" often arises. Pictures and charts may help or hinder according to their presentation. In showing a picture before or after the story, preface it with, "He was a big giant like the one in this picture," not, "I'll show you a picture now." Keep all aids an integral part of your one impression.

Amy Carmichael abandoned all use of pictures in her work in India, because the children's imagination seemed more satisfying. "I thought Jesus was lovelier than that," one boy told her after she had shown a picture. Marie Shedlock preferred only one stimulus at a time.

> I have come to the conclusion that the appeal to the eye and the ear at the same time is of doubtful value, and has, generally speaking, a distracting effect: the concentration on one channel of communication attracts and holds the attention more completely.[5]

Simple flannelgraph figures, maps, and model tabernacles may be used effectively if you do not stop unwinding the narrative to show the illustration. However, the elaborate, large felt characters available for flannelgraphs are often so beautiful that children become more interested in the colorful dolls than in the story itself. Attention from the story itself must not be distracted.

Dr. Wade Smith very successfully illustrates his stories with his famous "Little Jetts." He draws the simple symbols while speaking, and his listeners fill in the details. So popular are his drawings, that his stories of the Bible and *Pilgrim's Progress* have been translated into other languages.[6]

Objects often suggest a truth. I once heard a very effec-

[5] *The Art of the Storyteller* (Reprinted through permission by Dover Publications, Inc., New York 10), p. 13f.
[6] See the *Sunday School Times* for the Little Jetts teaching the current Sunday School lesson.

tive story at a summer camp woven around an old dry stick picked up from the ground. Could God use even a stick? The incidents of the axe head that floated by a stick, of Aaron's rod that budded, of the widow with her oil, meal, and a few sticks, and finally of the sticks used for the Cross — all were developed into one unified impression not to be forgotten.

THE PALESTINE MAP SONG

Some like the group to sing this "Palestine Map Song" while a child draws the locations on the map. Draw a diagram on the blackboard similar to Part I of Chart IV. Draw in the coast line, the Sea of Galilee, and the towns while the song is being sung. The map will then resemble Part II of Chart IV.

Palestine Map Song

(Tune — "Maryland, My Maryland")

First the line of coast we make;
Merom next, a marshy lake;
Then the Sea of Galilee
Exactly east of Carmel, see?
The Jordan River flows through
To the Dead Sea on the south;
While the Great Sea westward lies,
Stretching far as sunset skies.

On Zion stands Jerusalem;
Six miles south is Bethlehem;
On Olive's slope is Bethany;
Bethabara by Jordan, see?
Our Saviour drank at Sychar's well;
Of boyhood days let Nazareth tell;
At Cana water turned to wine;
It showed our Lord to be divine.

Capernaum by Galilee;
Nearest twin, Bethsaida, see?
Caesarea Philippi
At Hermon's base is seen to lie;
Along the coast these three appear:
Gaza, Joppa, Caesarea;
South to Bethel we may go;
To Hebron next, and Jericho.

Diagram for "Palestine Map Song"

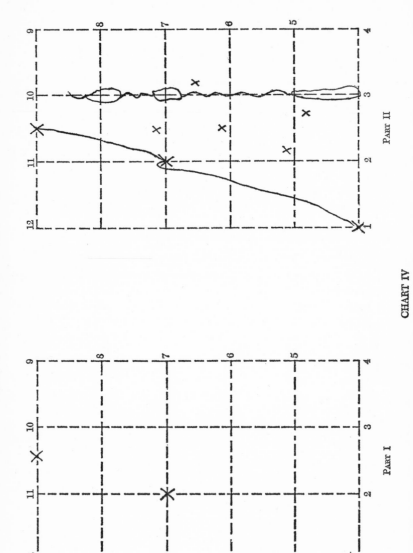

PART I

PART II

CHART IV

STORYTELLING 87

From heathen Tyre materials came
To build a temple to God's Name.
The sorrowing widow's son at Nain
Jesus raised to life again.
See Dan where Jordan's rivers rise,
Beersheba nearer tropic skies;
North and south these cities stand
To mark the length of Israel's land.

DISCUSSION SUGGESTIONS

1. Where would you find the geography and history of Old and New Testament times?
2. What complete stories may be found in the life of Joseph, Moses, or Paul?
3. Do you find Bible pictures helpful?
4. In what spirit should you approach the telling of a Bible story?
5. What Bible story books have you found helpful?

STIMULATING READING

BROWN, JEANETTE PERKINS. *The Storyteller in Religious Education.*
    VII. "Bible Stories"
    VIII. "Bible Stories: Stories of Jesus"
WIGHT, FRED. *Manners and Customs of Bible Lands.* Chicago: Moody Press, 1953.
MACKIE, GEORGE. *Bible Manners and Customs.* New York: Fleming H. Revell Co.
TERRIEN, SAMUEL. *Lands of the Bible.* New York: Simon and Schuster, 1957.
    (Children's Illustrated Edition)

SUGGESTED PROJECTS

1. List five Bible stories appropriate for each age group.
2. Write an introduction to two Bible stories.
3. Study the climate of Palestine in Chapter I of Mackie.
4. Suggest two different points of view for the same Bible story.
5. Adapt a Bible story for a certain period, and tell it to the class.
6. Make a list of helpful references, such as a Bible dictionary, history, geography, and biographies.
7. Prepare a story map of Palestine.

CHAPTER VIII

HOW TO PREPARE A STORY
FOR BROADCASTING

A democracy can extend only as far as the sound of a man's voice. — SOCRATES

Since teachers, librarians, and religious leaders are often expected to participate in local radio and television story hours for children, we should include a few suggestions for the broadcaster of stories. It is startling to realize that televiewing has become the favorite leisure activity of many elementary school pupils. They spend an average of 23.7 hours weekly watching programs. High school pupils teleview 14 hours. Today nearly every child has access to television but few stop to select the wheat from the tares.[1]

The opportunity for worth-while story broadcasts for children is very challenging. While boys and girls are often forced to share adult programs which encourage sophistication rather than extending the period of childhood, there are good story broadcasts for them. The rich field of children's literature should provide the main part of the content of their story hours and the main cues for handling plot and character development in the stories originating from other sources.

In a recent scientific study of television and youth, children were asked what programs on TV they would like more of. The first four answers were: stories of great heroes, great moments in history, stories of science, and well-known children's stories.[2]

Arthur I. Jersild, professor of education at Teachers College, Columbia University, and consulting psychologist in connection with Children's Radio Programs, Columbia

[1] Paul Witty, "A Sixth Report on TV," *School and Society* (April 15, 1956), Vol. 83, p. 166-168. (1955 statistics.)
[2] *Television and Youth* (Washington, D.C.: National Association of Radio and TV Broadcasters, 1954), p. 16. Used by permission.

Broadcasting System, recognized the importance of a child's listening hours when he said:

> The power of radio in the lives of children presents both a challenge and an obligation. Children make a huge investment of time in radio programs. They do this during years that are important in the development of their minds and emotions. Through the radio they extend the boundaries of their experiences and lift themselves beyond the horizons of their workaday world. They come mainly to be entertained, not to be educated. But the experiences they have by way of the radio contribute to the shaping of their ideas and attitudes, their interests, tastes, moral concepts, and habits of thought. This fact is challenging. It also puts upon each broadcast a share of the responsibility for the sum total of what the radio offers.[3]

CRITERIA FOR CHILDREN'S BROADCASTS

Broadcasting has had its successful storytellers for young listeners. Nila Mack, Isabel Hewson, Madge Tucker, Ireene Wicker, and Lydia Perera might head the list. To these could be added many who are particularly stressing the story with a purpose, exemplified by the story hours of "Aunt Theresa," "Aunt Bertha," "Uncle Dan and Aunt Sue," "Uncle Bob," and Mrs. Ethel Barrett.

Program requisites are similar to those already discussed. There must first of all be absolute clarity. Listeners are interested only in what they understand. This is achieved through simplicity of language, construction, and ideas appropriate for the age group to whom the story is slanted. In the second place, the story hour must hold interest. Fast-moving action, the use of dialogue, and human-interest appeals help to hold attention.

Nila Mack, Children's Director for the Columbia Broadcasting System, advised: "Don't forget that there is such a theory as a tired businessman of nine, and if history, geography, and botany have to creep into his listening hours, don't forget to let them creep."

Realizing the need for careful selection in listening hours, non-profit organizations such as the AMERICAN COUNCIL FOR BETTER BROADCASTS[4] and THE NATIONAL ASSOCIATION FOR

---

[3]Dorothy Lewis and Dorothy McFadden, *Program Patterns for Young Radio Listeners* (Washington, D.C.: National Association of Broadcasters, 1945), p. 1. Used by permission.
[4]423 N. Pinckney, Madison, Wisconsin.

BETTER RADIO AND TELEVISION,[5] are continually evaluating
radio-TV programming. Those interested may obtain their
releases of children's programs in a five-point rating from
excellent to most objectionable.

The standards for evaluating children's programs used
by NAFBRAT are based largely upon the criteria for children's radio and TV programs published by the United
States Office of Education. Basically, they require a balance
between three different aspects of the program, without
undue stress upon one at the expense of another as follows:

(1) Its portrayal of the moral and social ideals of American
life; i.e., faith in democracy, understanding and tolerance of
all races and creeds, principles of good taste and good character, and respect for law and order. It is important to note
here that crime is *never* suitable as the major theme of a
program for children.

(2) Its influence on the emotional and intellectual development of a child; i.e., avoidance of excessive emotional
stimulation and undue stress upon fear and aggression,
human rather than superhuman hero portrayals, a clear
differentiation between fantasy and fact, immediate resolu-
tion of suspense, respect for family and friends, introduction to new hobbies, interests, and knowledge, and humor
within the comprehension of the child.

(3) Standards of showmanship; i.e., good writing, acting
and direction; music and sound effects in keeping and not
excessively stimulating; vocabulary at the proper age level
and in good English except where a characterization requires colloquialisms; authenticity as to the historical or
factual information.[6]

THE SINGLE NARRATOR

The various types of story hours produced over the air
differ mostly in technique, from the single narrator to the
dramatized story. Ireene Wicker found that the generous
use of music and high contrasts in characterization helped
to hold interest. Her great popularity as "The Singing Lady"
has led to her programs being transcribed for the pleasure
and education of thousands of young children who did not
hear her in the past.

"Aunt Theresa" of WMBI uses the single narrator method.

[5] 882 Victoria Avenue, Los Angeles 5, California.
[6] "Look and Listen" (pamphlet), Radio and Television Guide to Better
Programs (Spring, 1958), prepared by the National Association for Better
Radio and Television, 882 Victoria Ave., Los Angeles, California. Used
by permission.

Mrs. Ethel Barrett, popular radio and TV storytelling artist, distinguishes her characters by tone and adds her own vocal sound effects in a continued story such as Bunyan's *Holy War*. On *Story to Order*, although the storyteller has always been the only voice, sound effects have accompanied the storyteller wherever appropriate, giving the story a partial dramatization. With some series, additional voices are used, but the storyteller must not drop from the scene for any long period.

These storytellers often present poetry, associating it with leisure, fun, and entertainment, not just a subject to be studied in school. The poems chosen are easily visualized and the words clearly understood. After a series of radio poetry periods over a Cleveland station, boys and girls of the upper grades who had not liked poetry before were bringing in poems that they had recently discovered and liked.

Except for two factors, the preparation of the story for broadcast is very much the same as that for the direct audience. In the first place, stories must be accurately tailored to the time allotted. If the story selected is not of the right length, it may have to be condensed or enlarged. There is no extra minute to round out the ending. The storyteller must practice it several times, keeping a record of the time required until it is of the desired length.

In the second place, the radio storyteller must depend entirely on the ear in getting a response. His voice must do the whole job. Tones must be pleasant and well-modulated. More attention must be given to the aural elements of sound words, euphony, and variety of interpretation. A child often tunes in to the personality of the storyteller, not to the program.

The TV storyteller must be more conscious of setting. One librarian friend holds the book from which the story is told. With three or four children seated around her, the story audience was complete. Her program director advised her always to wear a full skirt that would fall gracefully about her.

Eulalie Steinmetz Ross, director of work with the children of the Public Library of Cincinnati, Ohio, used this narrator

method on her TEL-A-STORY TV program over WCET
on the city's first educational TV station. With several children from branch libraries as a studio audience, and occasionally props and music when they "honestly extended
the meaning of the story told," she told her stories. From
this eleven-months' project, she learned that the story hour
should be prepared with simplicity, and that the storyteller
should be pleasant to listen to and to look upon, enjoying
the story herself. She found the personality of the storyteller to be of major importance. Special birthdays were
honored and the wishing candle lit for Beatrix Potter, Hans
Christian Andersen, Marie Shedlock, and other story favorites. This program so popular with fourth and fifth graders
was discontinued only when the telecast hours were
changed.[7]

THE DRAMATIZED STORY

Such popular story hours as *Let's Pretend, The Children's
Bookshelf,* and *Your Story Hour* are developed by dramatization with different individuals taking the character parts.
Most of these programs are reproductions of the great
stories of literature. The nature stories of Thornton Burgess
and biographies of great leaders have been so presented.

Typical of the story with a purpose is the program produced by "Aunt Bertha" in her *Children's Bible Hour,*
originating at Grand Rapids, Michigan, but transcribed over
many radio and TV stations in both the United States and
in foreign mission stations. Always she includes a fifteen-
minute story illustrating some Bible truth. Most of the
characters are portrayed by the children who participate in
the weekly broadcast.

Your Story Hour, produced in Medina, Ohio, but also
transcribed in half the states and in several foreign countries, has as its slogan: "Making boys and girls of today
better men and women of tomorrow." "Uncle Dan and Aunt
Sue" tell the story with the help of others on dialogue parts,
but keep the thread of the story.

The preparation of a story with its various character
parts differs mostly from the single narrator story in tech-
nical form. Follow the format of a radio script as found

[7]Eulalie Steinmetz Ross, "Hints from a TV Storyteller," *Library Journal*
(April 15, 1956), Vol. 81, p. 981-984.

at the end of this chapter. Keep all the characters listed at the left of the page, and underline the music or sound effects so that each may be easily identified.

In content, remember that the radio story is heard by ear and must appeal to the imagination for scenery. Put the stage directions in the words of the characters. Instead of writing *(Don leaves to the right)*, have Sallie call, "So you are leaving? Good-by!" As in the narrated story, much is implied by tone of voice, pause, and inflection without exposition.

Change of scenes may be indicated by several methods. A musical bridge or the ticking of a clock often suggest the passage of time. The narrator may use exposition. Try to limit the number of scenes. Keep the action moving. Give the characters short dialogue parts, not long speeches. In adapting a classic story, preserve the original conversation as much as possible.

A few appropriate sound effects as the opening of a door, the crushing of a piece of cellophane for fire, or the rhythmic beat of a pencil on sandpaper for the gallop of a horse, add to a sense of reality. Characters fade in and out to suggest distance. Timing to a split-second finish is demanded by all broadcast productions. Practice carefully for quality of tone, characterization, and interpretation.

Although these media can never replace the direct personal contact of the storyteller with his listeners, storytelling with a purpose may be a powerful force for good as well as wholesome entertainment over both radio and television. Roger Babson's prediction is still true, "Radio offers as great an opportunity for a new era of religious and educational renaissance as did the printing press three centuries ago."

DISCUSSION SUGGESTIONS

1. Contrast the method of the storyteller directly before his audience with that of the storyteller on the air.
2. What worthwhile stories have you heard broadcast?
3. Name several storytelling artists of radio or TV.
4. What can you do to encourage your local station to produce desirable story hours?
5. What are the values and opportunities of a storyteller on a broadcast?
6. Evaluate the criteria of a children's broadcast.

STIMULATING READING

Ross, Eulalie Steinmetz. "Hints from a TV Storyteller," *Library Journal* (April 15, 1956), Vol. 81, p. 981-984.

Abbott, Waldo and Rider, Richard. *Handbook of Broadcasting.* New York: McGraw-Hill Book Co., Inc., 1957.
    XV. "The Preparation of Programs for Children."

Emerson, Laura S. "Aunt Bertha," *Moody Monthly* (April, 1954), Vol. 54, No. 8, p. 43.

SUGGESTED PROJECTS

1. Listen to a children's story hour noting the broadcast techniques.
2. Study the radio script given at the end of this chapter.
3. Choose a story for dramatic presentation.
4. Adapt this story in script form and plan the sound effects and music.
5. Present the story to the class.
6. Obtain a list of the better broadcasts for children from the two non-profit organizations referred to in this chapter.

"Reuben and His Queer Moccasins" *

And now here is Aunt Sue with another Indian story called "Reuben and His Queer Moccasins."
(Music: sneaks in)

The story about Reuben's queer moccasins that I'm about to tell takes place in the East . . . during the thirteen-colony period of America's history. It happened not far from where the present city of Providence, Rhode Island, now stands.
(Music: up-under)

Aunt S.:   It is a cold winter day. The wind howls *(Sound: wind)* around the corners of a certain log cabin, making deep drifts of the driving, whirling snow. *(Sound: wind fades)* Inside the cabin, a cherry fire burns *(Fire)* in a wide fireplace. . . . Over in a corner of the cabin, a bed *(Fire fades)* had been made for a very sick lady, Grandma Gage. . . . Granddaughter Dorothy stands at the foot of the bed, her seven-year-old face showing

*Written and produced over YOUR STORY HOUR by Virgil Iles, Medina, Ohio. Used with permission.

very serious and troubled thought. Standing erect and tall by the side of Grandma's bed is Dorothy's thirteen-year-old brother Reuben. Both Dorothy and Reuben are listening intently to Grandma Gage.

(*Music: out*)

(Sound: fire is in background)

GRANDMA: I wish with all my heart that I were back in England. I was too old when I came here to America to adjust myself to the new world and new way of life.

DOROTHY: You're not old, Grandma.

GRANDMA: I'm very old, Dorothy . . . and about to die. If only I could see my two sons just once more, I would die satisfied and in peace.

REUBEN: Father'll be back any day now, Grandma . . . maybe today.

GRANDMA: No, Reuben, your father was going by to see your uncle before he came home.

REUBEN: Want me to go to Uncle Nathan's and get Father and Uncle Nathan?

GRANDMA: No, Reuben . . . It's way too far for a boy to walk in this kind of weather.

REUBEN: I'm not a boy and I wouldn't walk. I'd skate on the river most of the way. I could easy get there before dark.

DOROTHY: But those mean Indians would get and scalp you.

GRANDMA: Indians? What Indians, Dorothy?

DOROTHY: The Indians that that man told us about.

GRANDMA: Reuben, have you and Dorothy been keeping something from me?

REUBEN: A . . . it isn't anything, Grandma. The man from Tar Hollow came by yesterday and told us it looks like maybe the Indians are getting ready to go on the warpath, that's all.

GRANDMA: Reuben, you should have told me. A . . . listen, you and Dorothy, I don't want either of you to venture beyond the well until your father gets back. Indians may be lurking out there in the woods just waiting for the chance to scalp you.

Now I — I'm awfully tired; go over there by the fireplace and let me nap for a spell.

REUBEN: All right, Grandma. Come on, Dorothy.
             (Sound: two pair footsteps on floor, fire coming in. Footsteps stop when fire is on Mike)

DOROTHY: *(Undertone)* Is Grandma going to die, Reuben?

REUBEN: I guess so. That's why I just gotta go to Uncle Nathan's and get Father and Uncle Nathan.

DOROTHY: *(Undertone)* But Grandma said not to go farther'n the well.

REUBEN: *(Undertone)* I didn't promise I wouldn't.

DOROTHY: *(Undertone)* But the Indians'll get and scalp you if you do.

REUBEN: *(Undertone)* I'll be careful. I'll walk down the road until I get to Walnut Creek. Then I'll cut across the ridge and down to Podunk Pond. I'll put on my skates there and skate across the pond and down Chicopee River to Uncle Nathan's.

DOROTHY: *(Undertone)* But what if the Indians do get you?

REUBEN: *(Undertone)* I've got to take that chance. Anyway, they won't . . ., not if both of us pray about it and trust God to take care of us.

DOROTHY: *(Undertone)* I'll pray every minute you're gone.

REUBEN: *(Undertone)* Thank you, Little Sis. And I'd better get started if I'm going to get there before dark. You go out to the shed and get my skates and that old gun while I put on my duds.

DOROTHY: *(Undertone fading)* All right.
             (Music: Covers, bridge)   *(Sounds: fire)*

DOROTHY: *(Coming in)* Here's your gun and skates, Reuben.

REUBEN: *(Undertone)* Shhh, not so loud; you'll waken Grandma and then she won't let me go.

DOROTHY: *(Undertone)* Be careful with that gun.

REUBEN: Don't worry, Little Sis, it isn't loaded. Be sure and keep the fire going and door bolted until I get back.

DOROTHY: I will.

REUBEN: And take good care of Grandma. I'll be back tomorrow with father and Uncle Nathan. Goodbye, Little Sis.

DOROTHY: Goodbye. And do be careful.
(Music: Covers Establish — Under)

AUNT S.: Reuben slung his skates over his shoulder, the old gun in the crook of his arm and started bravely down the snow-covered road...*(Sound: wind, footsteps in snow)* He walked as fast as he could, . . . keeping sharp watch to the right and left for signs of Indians. . . . He reached Walnut Creek without incident. Then he cut across rough fields and through thick woods until he reached the top of the ridge. There he stopped *(Footsteps stop)* . . . and looked around him in every direction.

REUBEN: *(To self)* I can see miles and miles from up here. Down there is Podunk Pond and over there . . . was that something moving? Maybe it's an Indian. *(Pause)* I guess it wasn't anything, after all. But I'd better get going before I do see Indians and they see me. *(Sound: Footsteps again in snow)*

AUNT S.: So Reuben started down the slope towards Podunk Pond. He was almost there when suddenly an arrow whizzed past his head. *(Sound: Arrow whizzing past and sticking in tree. Footsteps in snow stop)*
(Music out)

REUBEN: *(To self)* Indians!

INDIANS: *(In distance. They start to yell, etc., coming in.)*

REUBEN: *(To self)* If I run fast, maybe I can get to the pond before . . . aw, aw, Indians all around me. I'm surrounded by Indians. A . . . Dear Jesus, help me to be brave. And protect me from the Indians if it is Thy will. Thank you. Amen.

INDIANS: *(Indians are now on Mike, all around Reuben.)*

REUBEN: *(Trying to be brave)* Be careful with those tomahawks, fellows.

INDIANS: *(Continue right on with their yelling, etc.)*

REUBEN: *(Desperately)* Please, fellows, . . . a . . . you no understand English?

PRINCE: Him Chief: Me his son. Him no understand English. Me do.

REUBEN: Glad to meet you, Prince. But, if it's all the same to you, I'd better get going now. Good-by.

PRINCE: You no go. Paleface scalp red men. Now red men scalp paleface.

REUBEN: What do you want my scalp for, Prince? It ain't no good.

PRINCE: Before we scalp paleface, me take thunder-stick.

REUBEN: This gun? Sure, sure, you can have it. It's no good to me now.

PRINCE: Me point thunder-stick at paleface . . . it go boom.

REUBEN: Not that thunder-stick, Prince. . . . It ain't loaded.

PRINCE: Me see. *(Sound: Click of gun hammer)*

REUBEN: Whew, I'm glad it wasn't loaded.

PRINCE: Thunder-stick no good. We scalp paleface now.

REUBEN: Just a minute, Prince, don't get mad. I got something else here you may have. Here. See? Nice, eh? You may have it.

PRINCE: Mmmm, sharp . . . scalp paleface with this.

REUBEN: No, no, Prince, that's a hunting knife, not a scalping knife.

PRINCE: It scalp paleface, anyhow.

REUBEN: Yes, but a . . . here, Prince, would you like this? *(Sound: ticking)*

PRINCE: What it?

REUBEN: It's a watch . . . keeps time.

PRINCE: Me take.

REUBEN: *It's yours,* Prince. With it you can tell the time . . . and it's time I'm going. Good-by.

PRINCE: What paleface have there?

REUBEN: This?

PRINCE: Ugh.

REUBEN: That, Prince is a-a-a-ice-moccasin.

PRINCE: What him for?

REUBEN: Ice-moccasins, Prince, are to walk on, walk across the ice with them.

PRINCE: Me no trust paleface.

REUBEN: I no trust you, either. A . . . maybe you want to walk on the ice, yes?

PRINCE: Me no trust ice-moccasin. But young brave here, he try. Paleface show brave how to use ice-moccasin?

REUBEN: Sure, Prince. Only we'll all have to go down where the ice is. Come on.

PRINCE: Ugh . . . but we watch you . . . you no escape.

REUBEN: *(Sighs)* Yes, I know.
            (Music: bridge)
            (Sound: wind)
            (Sound: Wind. Also sounds that match the following speech)

REUBEN: All right, Brave stick out your foot. That's it. Now, I just fasten this skate to your foot . . . like this. Ah, it fits. Now, your other foot. See, there's no mystery about it — *(To self)* yet. *(To Indian)* Now, all you gotta do is stand up and walk — *(To self)* if you can. *(To Indian)* Here, let me help you up. There, now walk!
            (Sound: Few steps on ice; then, kerplunk, down he goes.)

INDIANS: *(Laugh)*

REUBEN: *(Laughing)* Tell him to try again, Prince.

PRINCE: Him mad. Him kill paleface.

REUBEN: Tell brave this all in fun.

PRINCE: Other braves laugh at him . . . him mad . . . him kill paleface.

REUBEN: Tell him that paleface put on ice-moccasin and let braves laugh at him.

PRINCE: You make braves laugh?

REUBEN: You bet I can, me make braves split sides laughing . . . , I hope. Just give me the skates and I'll show you. Ha-Ha-Ha.
            (Music: Bridge) (Sound: Wind. Putting skates on)

REUBEN: There, they're on.

PRINCE: Paleface walk on ice-moccasins now?

REUBEN: Me try, Prince.

PRINCE: Me and braves not let you escape . . . form ring around you.

REUBEN: Go ahead, Prince. *(To self)* That's what I was afraid of. Oh, well, I'll stumble around, make them laugh at me. . . . Maybe something'll happen to give me a chance to escape. *(To Indians)* All right, Prince, here I go.

INDIANS: *(Talk, etc., during the following)*

INDIANS: *(Laughs)*

REUBEN: *(To self)* I wish they'd laugh so hard they'd forget to watch me so closely. Well, here goes again.
             (Sound: Few steps on skates, then kerplunk down)

INDIANS: *(Laugh)*
             (Music: Covers establish — under)

AUNT S.:   Reuben got up and fell again . . . and again. The Indians laughed with delight. Reuben gradually skated a little back and forth and around the circle of Indians. The circle got a little larger each time. Reuben continued to get up and fall . . . get up and fall. The Indians continued to laugh, they laughed so hard they relaxed their guard a little, and Reuben, watching for an opening, suddenly made a turn and, like a streak of lightning, took off across the pond with all the speed his young legs and hope could muster.
             (Music: Out)   *(Sound: Fast skating)*

REUBEN: *(To self)* I fooled 'em. I hope I can get out of arrow range before they realize what happened and start shooting at me.

INDIANS: *(In near distance. They yell. Gradually fades)*

REUBEN: *(To self)* They're after me. I don't dare take time to look back.
             (Music: Covers establish — under)

AUNT S.:   Reuben skated swiftly, expertly across the pond, then down the river, keeping as far as possible away from the trees and bushes along the river's edge. Finally, he arrived at his uncle's and found his father there. When told of Reuben's experience, they sent messengers out in every direction to warn the settlers of danger. Then, at daybreak the next morning, Reuben, his father, and his uncle mounted swift horses and started for the little cabin where brave Dorothy and sick Grandma awaited their arrival.

(Music: Up — under)

AUNT S.: Somehow, they arrived at the cabin without encountering any hostile Indians. Grandma Gates was still alive and smiling.

(Music: Out)

GRANDMA: *(Chuckles)* I'm mighty glad you made it safely, Reuben. And I'm mighty glad to see my two sons again . . . Now I can die in peace.

JOHN: You'll be living around for many a month yet, Mother.

GRANDMA: No, I won't John, my son.

NATHAN: Sure you will, Mother.

GRANDMA: No, Nathan, no. I've run my race, now I'm at the end. I'm ready to go. And, thanks to a brave grandson, I'm contented and happy.

REUBEN: I didn't do anything, Grandma.

DOROTHY: Please don't go away, Grandma.

GRANDMA: I have to, Dorothy. And, you're brave, too. Fact is, I'm mighty proud of both my grandchildren, mighty proud.

(Music: Sneaks in — up — under)

AUNT S.: This story about Reuben and his queer moccasins is a true story. . . . It actually happened. The Indians in the story are real. Later, they built a fortification near Podunk Pond. Many a generation has passed since then, but that old fortification still stands. It's known as Fort Hill. And the children of that neighborhood, as they play *(Sound: Children playing)* around that old fort and dig up Indian arrowheads, are told and retold the true story of how Reuben bravely faced his savage captors and, using his queer ice-moccasins, made his escape across the frozen waters of Podunk Pond and down Chicopee River.

(Music: Up to end of segue to finale)

CHAPTER IX

HOW TO ARRANGE A STORY HOUR

I would rather be the children's storyteller than the queen's favorite or the king's counsellor.
— KATE DOUGLAS WIGGIN

"I've checked out the book with the story in that you told us last week," volunteered Janie to the librarian after the story hour. "I want to read more like that one!" This stimulation to read is one of the greatest by-products of the story hour conducted in most city libraries. Kindergarten and elementary teachers are scheduling the story hour as an integral part of the program. The National Recreational Association also advocates story hours on playgrounds and in camp activities where stories become a social and moral force.

Religious educators are realizing that the story hour is a potential power in its teaching ministry, and they are taking the story to those who do not attend church. Forgotten ideals are renewed in the Christian summer camp, Sunday School classes, foreign-speaking centers, and the Good News Clubs. In detention homes and hospitals, the storyteller takes his healing balm pointing to a higher life.

The story hour should be a carefully planned activity if it is to be successful. This preparation will be discussed under (1) Principles of Arrangement, (2) Use of Poetry, and (3) Use of Art and Music.

PRINCIPLES OF ARRANGEMENT

Time and Place. The popular phrase, "story hour," does not accurately refer to the length of time given to a period of storytelling. Because of time-fatigue, sixty minutes is considered a full period for the older children or adults.

Twenty or thirty minutes will be long enough for concentrated listening for the pre-school groups.* It is better to leave listeners eager for more stories than to tire them out with too many.

Story hours may be conducted anywhere — under a big shady tree, on the steps of the shelter house, or in a classroom with a screen concealing the everyday tasks. Privacy, intimacy, leg room, and fresh air are the principal ingredients. Keep the seating comfortable whether you use chairs or "story rugs." Children need to be physically close and in direct range of the teller's eyes, in order to be mentally close. An attractive place with pictures, flowers, or wishing candle, will command greater attention. Try to keep the group small. Telling a story to more than thirty is difficult unless the storyteller is very skilled. Twenty near enough to hear without straining is more desirable.

You may gain prestige by naming your place the "Make-Believe Corner," "The Story Tree," or the "This Is His Life Hour." Picture Book Hour and Story Hour tickets are issued by many librarians. The tickets, which are free, help to control the number, and add to the importance of the hour.

Candle Ceremony. Since it is desirable to have "hushed quiet" before beginning the story hour, atmosphere can be created by using a record player, music box, a familiar chorus, or candles. Mrs. Augusta Baker, Storytelling Specialist of the New York Public Library, suggests this candle ceremony:

> The candle is lit at the beginning of the story hour in order to gain the undivided attention of the audience. "When the candle is lit, all talking must stop," says the storyteller. At the end of the story hour wishes are made, silently, and the audience blows towards the candle, held by the storyteller. "Do not leave your seats because, if you do, your wishes will be lost." Sometimes, there are two candles — one for wishes for someone else and one for wishes for one's own self.
> A librarian, at the end of the story hour, selects a boy and a girl from the audience to serve as "blowers." At the same time the audience recites this little rhyme:

*Summer story hours are shorter because it is difficult for children to sit still too long in hot weather. The length of the hour ultimately depends on the listening capacity of the audience.

"Story candle, bright and gay,
Grant this wish I make today."[1]

Number of stories and their order. Some authorities recommend three stories for the story hour. The first story is usually shorter in length, from five to ten minutes, dependent upon the listeners. It may be a wholesome story of humor or of human interest in which the listeners will be oriented at once. A story of atmosphere easily gains attention and holds interest.

The second story may be longer and more thoughtful and dramatic. This story suggests the message appealing to reason and to the emotions. In contrast, the third story is shorter, a relaxing story of charm which leaves a good impression. Be sure that the last story is satisfying and easily comprehended while the second is still being mentally assimilated. The climax of the story hour should be about two-thirds of the way through the program. If there is a wide range in age, choose a simpler story first for the younger children who may then be dismissed. Follow with two longer ones for the older.

However, the number of stories told will vary from just one to five or six, depending on the occasion and the circumstances. A good story hour is built upon an over-all balance with shorter stories interspersed with longer ones, and a blend of various moods from humor to pathos in both familiar and new stories.

For younger children it is wise to divide the story hour with a rest period such as some swinging game or finger play. Let the children stand up and relax by stretching out their arms as an airplane, bird, or some suitable pantomime. This may be done to music. A motion chorus accomplishes this same purpose.

Try rising and sitting in this activity exercise sung to the tune of "The Farmer in the Dell."

There was a king on earth
Who had a thousand men,
And every hill he led them up,
He led them down again.

[1]From *Once Upon a Time* (pamphlet), prepared by the New York Library Association (1955), p. 9. Used with permission.

Now when they're up, they're up,
And when they're down, they're down,
But only when they're half way up,
They're neither up nor down.

Seek to keep everyone listening and doing together. The storyteller will not want to use negative suggestion by asking if the children are tired. Just direct them in the exercise planned. Always emphasize the story rather than the play.

Theme. Every story hour should center around one dominant theme or impression. Such a similar purpose will unite varied stories so that they will produce a single effect just as the individual story does. Themes may be many and varied, ranging from character traits, such as courage, kindness, honesty, or helpfulness, to animals, flowers, toys, or music. Children like stories about Indians, foreign lands, missionaries, explorers, inventors, scientists, and doctors. Special days as Christmas, Easter, Spring, Autumn, Thanksgiving, or patriotic holidays, call for appropriate themes.

Marie Shedlock liked to plan a story hour around an author or country, using the folk tales of Hans Christian Andersen or the tales of India. A program of all Bible stories, of Uncle Remus' stories, or of hero tales will appeal to various age groups. Birthdays of heroes or authors may be celebrated with stories and poems about or by the special character.

Variety. Stories should be selected with perspective, a proper blend of humor and sentiment or fantasy and realism. After choosing an appropriate theme, attain variety through both (1) change of mood and (2) type of story. Moods may shift from humor to pathos, from romance and charm to adventure and morality. By using careful transitions, you may go from make-believe to true stories of biography, nature, or the story of a song or picture. Combine the classical favorites from great fiction, epics, legends, and fables with the more recent mechanical, scientific, and travel story.

A well-balanced story hour may have all these various elements, and yet contain stories of purpose to meet the standards of a good story. The story hour on courage should include more than physical bravery alone as portrayed in the story of the "Leak in the Dike" or of David and Goliath. Franklin D. Roosevelt or Fanny Crosby overcoming their handicaps also depicts courage. The moral courage of the Three Hebrew Children in refusing to yield their convictions or of Patty in "The Watch That Disappeared"[2] is just as necessary in rounding out the theme of courage.

In order to keep a true perspective, a story hour centered around Indians must show more than those fought by Daniel Boone. Include such prominent Indians as the Christian opera singer, Chief White Feather, who sang for the King and Queen of England when they were at the White House, or the war hero who helped to raise our flag on Iwo Jima.

Spencer G. Shaw, specialist in storytelling at the Brooklyn, New York, Public Library, has originated a method of correlating literature and music in programs of storytelling. The universal arts of poetry, music, and art serve to enhance the story hour.

USE OF POETRY

In her delightful record of her family's pleasures with books, Annis Duff relates her eight-year-old daughter's appreciation of the poetry of the Psalms.

Once, on the day of the first snow, we read together the One Hundred and Forty-seventh Psalm, because of the memorable verse, "He giveth snow like wool, and scattereth the hoarfrost like ashes." Out of that came one of the warmest tributes I have ever had: the children in our daughter's grade at school were discussing which of two psalms they should choose to memorize for a Thanksgiving exercise, and our representative cast her vote for "O give thanks unto the Lord," "because," she explained, "I already know 147." "I'll bet you don't," came the challenge. And away went the challenged:

"Praise ye the Lord, for it is good to sing praises unto our God.

"For it is pleasant, and praise is comely.

"The Lord doth build up Jerusalem, he gathereth together . . ."

"All right, all right, you know it! How?"

"My mother read it to me that day it snowed."

"You mean your mother *reads you the Bible?*"

"Of course," this without a trace of swagger or self-consciousness. "My mother reads me all the good books."

[2]See Part II.

How pleasant to have an eight-year-old accept the Bible, so rich a source of magnificent poetry, as a *good book!*[3]

Children have a natural response to poetry. Poetry should be recited or read at every story hour — not only poetry written especially for children, but the world's great poetry. In just a few lines a poet may depict an emotion or truth expressing the experience of the child. Joseph Auslander once wrote: "I am Poetry. . . I am the most beautiful way of remembering what it would impoverish you to forget." Poetry has been defined as the expression of one world in terms of another. Good poetry stretches the mind and implants lasting truths. When well chosen, poetry read or recited aloud gives a child a happy experience and makes an effective transition from one story to another. Only when poetry is not read well or is analyzed, do children dislike it.

Children have an innate sense of rhythm. They enjoy poetry because of its swinging, rhythmic movement which sings its way into their imagination. Youngsters like to beat out the poetic pattern. Poetry is characterized not only by cadence, but by tonal quality. Pleasing sound effects are found in alliteration, rhyme, figurative language, and the onomatopoeias which "clash," "sizzle," and "hiss." Its imagery abounds in sensory appeals to sight, hearing, smelling, touching, tasting, and the kinesthetic sense of movement. The iambic meter expresses serious moods, and the trochaic happy emotions.

Poetry may become an enriching contribution to the story hour. Since Christina Rossetti and Robert Louis Stevenson pioneered in writing poetry especially for children, the treasury of children's verse is continually being increased. In what better way could a story hour on Indians be introduced than with Annette Wyatt's "Indian Children"? The rollicking rhyme of Henry van Dyke's "The Foolish Fir Tree" delightfully encloses a lesson in contentment. The reactions of today's child are expressed poetically in Christopher Morley's "Animal Crackers," Rachel Field's "Taxis," and A. A. Milne's "Half Way down the Stairs."

In addition to the lyric poetry, many longer, narrative

[3]*Bequest of Wings* (New York: The Viking Press, 1946), p. 75. Used with permission.

poems may be told as those from the "Song of Hiawatha" or the great epic of Beowulf. John Masefield's story without an end, "Minnie Maylow's Story," always brings a joyous response. "Paul Revere's Ride" is still a favorite. Older listeners are interested in a story from the life of a poet about his verse. How William Cullen Bryant's faith in God's guidance was realized, is firmly expressed in his classic "To a Waterfowl." The storyteller may like to read a ballad and let the listeners join in reciting the refrain.

USE OF MUSIC AND ART

Each of these related arts may be woven into the story hour. When William Congreve wrote, "Music hath charms to soothe the savage breast," he probably did not have a story hour in mind. Nevertheless, appropriate record music while the children are gathering or leaving, will help to quiet voices. We are accustomed to identifying our favorite radio story hours by the musical theme.

Records may also help to create the atmosphere of the story hour — a stirring march or national anthem for the patriotic program, the "Parade of the Wooden Soldiers" for the theme on toys, or sacred hymns for the Bible story group. Older groups may want to participate in the singing, a cappella, as part of the opening of the story hour. When telling the story of some opera, hymn, or carol, give an audible illustration by producing part of it. In a summer youth camp I frequently augmented my course in Hymnology with group participation of the hymns studied.

Pre-school and kindergarten children will appreciate the Picture-Book Hour. Seat the listeners on chairs or individual story rugs for comfort and good viewing. As the storyteller turns the pages toward the children, they will follow the action and movement with anticipation. Beautiful illustrations and colors in many editions hold an aesthetic value as well.

We have already referred in Chapter VII to the use of visual aids, such as the flannelgraph. Pictures by the great artists such as Tate's "Boyhood of Raleigh," Millet's "The Angelus," or Breton's "Song of the Lark," have their place when woven into the context of the hour. Religious leaders

Theme: GOD'S CARE
Music: "The Lord Is My Shepherd" or "My Sheep Know My Voice"
Decorations: Pictures of Palestine — sheep
Programs: Sheep silhouette
Stories: "A Lesson of Faith"[11]
       "Tinny, Tin, Tin!"[11]
       "The Shepherd"[11]
Poem: Psalm 23 read chorically

CHILDREN AS TELLERS

The question is often asked, "Should children tell stories themselves?" Yes, storytelling is a two-way activity. Children may profitably tell their own favorite stories. I visited one of my former students on educational day during her first year of teaching. As representative children chosen from her third-grade class told their stories, the parents listened in surprise and pride at their poise and appreciation. Another student made storytelling a part of his sophomore English class, reporting very gratifying results.

Grade children often organize into a Storytelling Club. Whittier School, Washington, D.C., for example, has used the story as a daily feature in each classroom since 1938. Children from kindergarten tots through ebullient sixth-graders volunteer to tell their chosen stories in the half-hour program. Discussion and suggestions for improvement based on previously developed criteria follow. A Story Festival is held in the spring with a storyteller selected from each room.

The National Recreation Association recommends a Story Club when storytelling is well done on the playground. An annual Storytelling Contest is set up with judges and prizes as part of the summer program.

A child's choice of story is often revealing, leading to a further understanding of his own personality likes and problems. The story may be an outlet for him as much as for an adult teller. By knowing children and guiding them carefully, storytelling will become an artistic activity *by* the children as well as *for* them.

DISCUSSION SUGGESTIONS

1. What story hours are held in your community?
2. Where could you introduce a story hour?
3. Why do children like or dislike poetry?
4. How should music become a part of the story hour?
5. To what extent should pictures be used with the story?
6. How would you go about organizing a story hour?

STIMULATING READING

COLINA, TESSA, (ed.). *Finger Plays and How to Use Them.* Cincinnati, Ohio: The Standard Publishing Co., 1952.

MOORE, ANNIE E. *Literature Old and New for Children.* New York: Houghton Mifflin Co., 1934.
  X. "Makers of Poetry for Children"

ADAMS, BESS PORTER. *About Books and Children.* New York: Henry Holt and Co., 1953.
  X. "Butter to My Bread"

JUNIOR LIBRARIES. (September - October, 1956), Vol. III, Nos. 1 and 2.

SUGGESTED PROJECTS

1. Select three stories around the theme of heroism. Of Indians.
2. Plan the appropriate poetry, music, and decorations for each story hour.
3. List five poems which could be used in a story hour. Read one aloud.
4. Interview your Children's Librarian regarding the local story hour.
5. Bring two art pictures which could be used in the story hour.
6. Tell a story to some shut-in or handicapped child.
7. Invite children in to enjoy your story hour.

Chapter X

HOW TO FIND STORIES

For him there's a story in every breeze, and a picture in every wave.

— Thomas Moore

Publishers are constantly turning out more and more literature for children. The storyteller's problem is that of selectivity. Stories with a purpose are often difficult to find. If they have a good moral truth, they may have a weak climax and structure, resulting in a "goody-goody" story which is not effective. Some of those which thrill and entertain do not uphold desirable ideals. The purposeful story, when found, may be told again and again with continued charm and delight.

Original Stories

The storyteller may wish to develop an incident into an original story in order to accomplish his purpose. One day while shopping, I glanced down and saw a little coin purse lying on the sidewalk. I picked it up, looked inside for the owner's name, and found only a twenty-dollar bill, some car keys, and a bank passbook. Since I was only a few doors from that bank, I gave the purse to the teller who asked my name, then promised to notify the owner. Two days later, a letter of thanks with two dollar bills arrived through the mail. With this incident as a basis, I wrote up the story for juniors and sent it to a religious publication.[1]

Watch for story material. A careful glance at current magazines and newspapers will often supply you with a germ-plot. A friend who writes professionally, says that she stimulates her mind by glancing through magazines at both pictures and stories. To find fresh ideas and images, look at

[1]"Victory through Song" is included in Part II.

an object or truth until you see something in it that you've never seen before.

To illustrate, I picked up a current issue of a religious periodical and found several significant news events that would make story material. Beany Hooper, the seven-year old Christian boy who was miraculously rescued from the bottom of a well was presented a Bible by the Rev. Billy Graham. The Auca woman who escaped from her tribe was brought with Rachel Saint to appear on the TV program, This Is Your Life. The chaplain taking the writer through Alcatraz told of two young men and their choices — one who chose the right, and the other who ended up in Alcatraz. These are just three possibilities in one little paper.

Most localities offer rich sources of historical anecdotes of Indians, pioneers, and heroes. Children particularly enjoy stories of the familiar — the places, markers, and statues of those they see daily. Local librarians are glad to help in collecting stories of locale. For example, the famous Frances Slocum Trail passes right through our community. The story of this little Quaker girl who was captured by the Indians in Pennsylvania and brought to Indiana where she married an Indian Chief and reared her family, is climaxed when she is finally found by her aging brothers and missionary nephew. At her request she was given a Christian burial at her death.

In many families there are anecdotes and stories as yet unprinted which serve to illustrate worthy points. Juniors are especially interested in personal events and the bio- graphical material of those they know. Some mothers repeat their exploits, telling the story in third person, rather than identifying themselves with the incident and lesson learned. Then there are legends handed down from family to family. This is how our folk tales have been preserved for us from mouth to mouth.

I've heard Ireene Wicker, the "Singing Lady" of radio fame, take a subject, such as chickens, and weave an inter- esting story around the facts — the number of eggs set yearly, the process of incubation, and the different kinds of chickens. Original material needs only to be recognized and evaluated.

Observe detail carefully. The first qualification of a creator of stories is keen observation. What do you see in your daily walk? What do you notice about people, their height, coloring, dress, mannerisms, and speech? You can train yourself to see and to report accurately as Thoreau did in Walden Pond and the Bronte sisters in their small community. Noah Carter, a converted gangster, tells that one of his first assignments in Chicago was to go to a certain address across the city, stand in the door of that room for two minutes, then return with an oral report on the location of the furniture and every exit.

Study an action picture for details. Imagine what led up to this situation and what might happen afterward. Out of this will grow the facts of the story. Without looking around, identify the pictures on the wall where you are, the dresses of the other girls, or the trees on the playground. Become an accurate observer.

Build a progressive structure. Review the principles of narration discussed in Chapter IV, then plan your story plot. Who and where are the characters? What obstacle or crisis do they face? How do they get out of trouble? These three questions summarize most of the incidents which lead to the climax of a well-rounded story. Be sure to keep the ending plausible as well as possible.

The germ of my story was found in my experience of finding a purse and receiving a reward, but there was no conflict. By creating a need for two dollars and then suggesting the ethical problem and temptation, two obstacles were overcome. We were satisfied when the character took the honest attitude, was able to pay her pledge, and received a dollar more than her need.

Religious leaders have a tendency to attach a very obvious moral to a story. Artistically the great truth should and can be woven throughout the whole story in the words of the characters themselves or in what is said about them. Keep the story natural, dramatic, and moving.

Should we encourage children to tell original stories? Boys and girls like to share their experiences. For relaxation with older children, let one start the story, then each add a part until the last one rounds out the story. If their stories are voluntary, not a "show-off," they aid in valuable expression.

While original stories have their place, they must not be substituted for the great stories of childhood. A person successful in spinning a personal yarn may do so at the exclusion of other stories which require more effort and advance preparation.

TYPES OF STORIES

In the last chapter, we suggested that the story hour program should include various stories, differing according to types of literature and structure as well as of theme and mood. Appropriate classified lists of children's stories are available in many references and from local librarians. Therefore we make no pretense of giving an exhaustive list of sources. It is our purpose to suggest only a few favorites to guide in the compiling of a personal collection of stories of purpose. Each of these stories is included in Part II.

Folklore — "The Frog" by Ruth Sawyer.

Folklore includes fables, myths, legends, animal and fairy tales. These depict the accumulated wisdom and universal emotions of everyday human beings. The tales are models of structure told in simplicity and directness. Although they are predominantly constructive in moral lessons, they must be selected with care. Ruth Sawyer found that "The Frog" was heard in more different forms than any other tale in old Spain. The Spaniard is one of the most dramatic storytellers. A true artist, no matter how many times he has told the story, tells it with a first-timeness. The refrain, "*Si Dios quiere*" (if God wills), expresses the theme of the story.

Classic Literature — "Sir Galahad" adapted from Malory's *Morte d'Arthur*.

Of all of the epics, romances, and tales of classical literature, there are few more inspiring than that of Sir Galahad of the Knights of King Arthur's Round Table. It has a wide appeal for both boys and girls, especially those in the Heroic Period. Here is a youth faithful to his king, and victorious in many adventures. "His strength was as the strength of ten, because his heart was pure." Art may be correlated with

STORYTELLING

the story by using George Watt's portrait of *Sir Galahad* portraying the youthful knight with the purposeful face, his white horse with the arched neck, and the protruding vines which seek to impede his upward way. The allegorical suggestion of youth on a quest for his king makes this a heroic story of purpose.

Bible Story — "The Fiery Furnace" adapted from Daniel III.

The Bible contains all the various types of stories — wonder, biographical, historical, romantic, and dramatic. They are told with directness and simplicity in such beautiful language that we wish to preserve the original purpose, atmosphere, and incidents. Natural reactions, sense appeals, and geographical conditions may be added for imagery. While some archaic words may need to be changed or explained, many expressions are so much a part of our language, as "burning, fiery furnace," that they are repeated again and again. "The Fiery Furnace" needs little rearranging in structure as the whole story is related in one chapter. However, a reference to Jewish training and the first two Commandments suggests why the young men would not bow. Bible stories are excellent examples of structure, diction, and teaching.

Biblical Background — "The Maid of Emmaus" by Agnes Sligh Turnbull.

Many profitable stories are built around Bible characters and scenes, especially the Christmas and Easter themes. Select those which do not weave in fictional incidents contrary to Bible teaching. This story of the little maid by an established author, presents a different viewpoint to a familiar truth.

Biographical Story — "The Boy Handel" by Laura S. Emerson.

Fortunately, many writers are preparing biographical stories for children. The fact that the incidents are true, appeals to children of many ages. If a story of a worthily successful person is accurately told in good style, it is invaluable. This true story, reprinted twice since its first publication, may be used for a Christmas, music, or a great-artist program.

Historical Story — "Betty's Ride" by Henry S. Canby.

Closely connected with the biographical is the story centering around historical events. Like the narrative with Bible background, details must be accurate in situation, costume, and diction. This story about a Quaker girl of the Revolutionary period contains enough action and suspense to hold the attention of boys and girls alike. Written by a well-known, short-story writer, it is appropriate for a patriotic or historic story hour.

Nature Story — "A Lesson of Faith" by Julia D. Cowles.

The wonders of creation are related in the many interesting nature and scientific stories now carefully written for children. Although trees and animals may talk in natural language, the facts must be accurate. Both knowledge and appreciation are increased. "It is perfectly legitimate," wrote John Burroughs, "for the animal storyteller to put himself inside the animal he wishes to portray, and tell how life and the world look from that point of view, but he must always be true to the facts of the case, and to the limited intelligence for which he speaks."[2] Julia D. Cowles has adapted an old, beloved story of Mrs. Margaret Gatty. When presenting a lesson on immortality as at Easter time, this principle observed in nature helps the child to understand everlasting life.

Mechanical Story — "Little Hector Helicopter" by Georgia Tucker Smith.

Twentieth-century children enjoy these animated, mechanized heroes typified by the ever popular, "The Little Engine That Could." This particular story is also a story poem — a read-aloud story in rhyme — with regular rhythm, euphony, and pleasing sound.

Holiday Story — "The Shining Secret" by Helen Frazee Bower.

Many story hours center around the special days. In the seasonal atmosphere with its music and decorations, the storyteller has an already-prepared effective setting. This particular Christmas story follows the original account from the Gospel of Luke, but is related from a heavenly point of

[2]"The Literary Treatment of Nature," *Atlantic Monthly,* Vol. 94, p. 38.

view, preserving the wonder, anticipation, and true purpose of Christmas. With its repetition of refrain and story pattern, it is easily memorized. I've found it a favorite with both children and adults.

Allegorical Story — "The Handful of Clay" by Henry Van Dyke.

Allegories, parables, and fables carry a second, higher meaning which is obvious, though indirect. Here Dr. Van Dyke uses the commonplace clay, yet clothes his message in beautiful language. This story helps us to understand the purpose of many of life's experiences. A playground or camp setting is appropriate for its telling.

Character-building Story — "The Watch That Disappeared" by Artie Appleton & Edith Warner.

While all stories of purpose contribute to personality growth, some are selected for definite character-building emphasis. The common experience and its consequences related in this story will help to influence character and conduct.

Missionary Story — "Tinny, Tin, Tin" by Laura S. Emerson.

Missionary stories are an accepted necessary part of religious education — those which are about missionaries and those which encourage missionary zeal. The jungle setting, elephants, and God's care — all elements from an actual experience — give this story a strong appeal. It can be used on an animal, foreign, or religious story hour.

Spiritual Story — "The Shepherd" by William MacKeller.

In religious education, we need some stories which reveal the plan and purpose of God without seeming preachy. Children like this particular story because of its Scottish setting, the sheep, and Sandy's question. It honors the ministry. It is only a step to comprehension of Christ, our Good Shepherd.

Adult Story — "The Guest of Honor" by Grace V. Watkins.

Because stories bring inspiration and release to adults as well as children, storytellers wisely include this type in their collection. Christian workers and the storyteller himself, will appreciate this understanding story of unsought reward.

Original Story — "Victory through Song" by Laura S. Emerson.

DISCUSSION SUGGESTIONS

1. How can you develop powers of observation?
2. Where can you find plots for original stories?
3. What are the benefits of inventing stories?
4. What will children gain by telling their own stories?
5. Is originality helped or hindered by preparation?

STIMULATING READING

ARBUTHNOT, MAY HILL. *Children and Books.* Chicago: Scott, Foresman and Co., 1957.

    pp. 580-617, Bibliography

JINNETTE, ISABELLA (ed.). *Stories to Tell.* Baltimore, Maryland: Enoch Pratt Free Library, 1956.

SUGGESTED PROJECTS

1. Report the results of one swift glance out of the window or in a strange room.
2. Bring to class a picture suggestion for a story. Analyze its conflict.
3. Outline the plot and purpose of the story in the picture.
4. Begin a picture scrapbook.
5. Prepare an original story.
6. Study bibliographies of different story types.
7. In what magazines could you find appropriate stories?
8. Add your own sources to those listed in the Bibliography in this text.

Part II
Fifteen Typical Stories to Tell

THE FROG*

In Spain one hears often the words: "*Si Dios quiere*" — If God wills. A simple person, especially a peasant, does not make plans without first saying it. To begin a journey, to go to market, to marry, or even to eat, it is well first to say: *Si Dios quiere,* a reminder that nothing can be accomplished unless God wills it.

This story of the frog I heard in different forms more often than any other in Spain.

Once there lived a peasant whom his neighbors called Perico. He had a small but fertile *finca.* He loved the earth; he raised the good carrots, the white onions, the excellent cabbages, and the green spinaches for those who liked them.

He had a wife and nine *pequenos;* and when there were vegetables left from the family table he took them to market and sold them for silver which bought many things that were needed.

One morning Perico woke early. "Today I am going to market," he told his wife.

"*Si Dios quiere* — if God wills," corrected his wife.

"There are a hundred carrots, a thousand onions, baskets of spinach. We need silver. I am going whether God wills or not."

All the time that he was putting the harness with brass bells and red tassels on Chorlito, the small gray donkey, and fastening him to the small two-wheeled cart, his wife stood at his side talking to him. "Husband, you must say it. Please. Say it even if you say it to no one but Chorlito."

"I will not say it. *Arre, burrito,*" he said to the donkey. He touched his ear with the end of his whip and they were off. His wife turned sorrowfully into the doorway. What was the use of shouting after him — "Go with God"? God would never follow the road with such a sinner.

Down the road that winds along the muddy river to Seville went Perico, the gray donkey, the little cart piled high with its baskets of vegetables. They fell in with another peasant, riding his donkey to be shod. "Where are you going?" he asked.

"I go to market."

*Reprinted from *Picture Tales from Spain,* by Ruth Sawyer. Copyright by J. B. Lippincott Co. Used with permission.

"Ay, truly you go to market — *Si Dios quiere.*"

"I go whether God wills or not," and Perico lashed Chorlito with the long whip.

They came up with a water-carrier who gave them good-day. "Where are you going?"

"I go to market."

"*Si Dios quiere* — yes?"

"I go whether God wills or not," shouted Perico.

They met the baker taking his hard, round loaves into the country to sell. They met the good *cura* going to baptize a new baby. They met a drove of gypsies on a pilgrimage. To each and all of them he shouted the same answer until he was hoarse, growing more hot and angry with each shouting. "I tell you — the world — for the hundredth time I go to market, to sell my vegetables, whether God wills or not!"

At the start of the bridge that crosses over the river from Triana to Seville he turned Chorlito up the incline and there he was stopped by a traveler with a long cape, well cloaking him, a wide hat of black beaver, shoes thick with the dust of the road, and a staff in his hand.

"Friend, where are you going?" he asked.

Perico looked at him with blazing eyes. "I go to market."

"*Si Dios quiere,* friend."

"Call me not friend; and I go whether God wills or not."

The traveler shot out an arm to stay him. "Today you speak as stupidly and stubbornly as a frog. Be a frog."

Before Perico could say — "*Basta!*" he found himself on the bank of the river, under the bridge; he was small, wet, green above, yellow underneath — a silly frog. Gone was Chorlito, beloved of donkeys, gone was the two-wheeled cart it had taken him a twelve-month to build, gone were the good carrots, the white onions, the excellent cabbages, the green spinaches, for those who liked them. He was a frog, accursed. He croaked aloud his misery: "*Ay de mi — ay de mi!*"

A heron flew up the river and screamed at him: "*Si Dios quiere, si Dios quiere, si Dios quiere.*"

Sailors on a ship docked nearby, pulled on the ropes of the rigging and sang together: "Ahoy — to the sea — *si Dios quiere — quiere — quiere.*"

The big bells on the *Giralda* rang out the hour: "Nine o'clock — *si Dios quiere.*"

The frog croaked his misery aloud again. "All of God's world is saying it but me," and he began to think of the wife and nine *pequenos* at home. "I must get back to them," he thought.

He began jumping up the bank, along the river, northwards. The going was slow — slow. A shadow fell on him, cutting off the sun. He looked far upwards. There stood the traveler, the cape on his shoulders, the hat on his head, the dust on his shoes, the staff in his hand.

"Senior Frog, where are you going?" he asked.

"Back to the wife and the nine *pequenos*."

"*Si Dios quiere,* yes?"

"Whether God wills or not, I go."

"Go if you must. You will find it a long journey for a frog."

And there he was, back at the bridge again, no distance home at all. He began his jumping along the river. The stones bruised his feet; the sun scorched his back. Noon had passed. He was getting nowhere. A shadow fell again upon him. Looking up he saw the traveler.

"And now, friend, where are you going?"

"Back to the nine *pequenos*."

"*Si Dios quiere?*"

"If God wills, yes."

"But I thought you were going to market?"

"To market, yes, if God wills."

"Good, And go with God."

Perico rubbed his eyes. Where was he? Was he going home? Was he going to market? Had he a gray donkey, Chorlito by name? Had he vegetables to sell? Was it morning — was it night?

He sighed enormously and with great content. He was no longer a frog. He was a man again, with a man's good legs under him. He was on the bridge, not under it. A loud heehaw shook the air at his elbow. God be praised — there was Chorlito, the two-wheeled cart, and the vegetables. He was Perico, the peasant, with a wife and nine *pequenos* waiting for him at home. *Basta!* He would buy them for a great surprise some *turron*, the good candy with its honey and almonds. But about the frog — he would keep that to himself.

SIR GALAHAD*

Adapted from Malory's
Morte d'Arthur

In the long, long ago, in the age of chivalry, when knights rescued those in trouble, King Arthur gathered his knights about the Round Table in the great hall at Camelot. There was only one large empty seat, "The Siege Perilous," which no knight had yet been worthy enough to occupy.

While the knights were recounting their adventures, a good old man clothed all in white, entered the hall. With him was a young knight, clad all in red, without sword or shield, but with an empty scabbard hanging by his side.

"Peace be with you, fair lords," greeted the good old man. Then he turned to speak to King Arthur. "Sir, I bring here a young knight of noble lineage who will work strange marvels in this court."

"He is right welcome," said King Arthur.

The good old man beckoned to the young knight, "Sir, follow me." He led him to the great covered seat next to the king. As he lifted up the cloth, he found engraved on the back of the seat, "This is the seat of Sir Galahad, the good knight."

All the knights started up in fright as the young knight sat down in "The Siege Perilous," for no one had ever dared sit in it before. When they realized that this young knight was named Sir Galahad, they sent up a shout which shook the hall. They knew that he was to do the greatest deeds of them all. Because his courage was great and his heart was pure, he would lead many to search for the Holy Grail. Then the good old man left.

Now Sir Galahad's sheath was still empty. One night the King took him by the hand and led the whole company down to the river where lay a great cube of marble with a sword driven into the middle of it. Several of the knights tried to draw out the sword, but it remained as firmly fixed as ever.

"You have no sword as yet, I see," said the King to Sir Galahad. "Do you try."

*Adaptation by Laura S. Emerson.

126

Sir Galahad stepped forward and easily drew the sword with its jeweled hilt from the stone and put it in the scabbard which hung from his side. It fitted exactly. Still more strange were the words inscribed upon the sword: "Never shall man take me hence, but only he by whose side I ought to hang, and he shall be the best knight of all the world."

As yet, Sir Galahad had no shield. He had been told that far away in the heart of the forest there was an old, old church in which was kept a snow-white shield with a cross of red in its center. Having lain there for centuries, it was invisible to everyone but the knight who could draw the jeweled sword from the block of marble. There Sir Galahad found his shield.

Although Sir Galahad was the youngest of the knights, he served the king faithfully. He proved himself to be steadfast and courageous. All the knights knew that "His strength was as the strength of ten because his heart was pure."[1] They also knew that only he who sat in "The Siege Perilous" would achieve the quest of the Holy Grail.

Now the Holy Grail was the cup or dish used by Christ at the Last Supper. For centuries it had been lost. Only he who was perfectly pure in thought, word, and deed would ever be able to find it. Many of the knights of King Arthur's Round Table searched for the Holy Grail. Some caught a passing vision of the mystic cup, but none ever possessed it.

When Sir Galahad started out on the quest of the Holy Grail, he had many adventures, but always won in every battle. He delivered Sir Melyas from the forest tempters who had caused him to forget his service to his king. He rescued the maidens who had been imprisoned in "The Castle of the Maidens" for seven long years. Still Sir Galahad rode on, doing many good deeds because he knew no fear and his heart was pure.

Now, at the year's end, Sir Galahad and two of the knights who had joined with him, had a vision of the Christ. As they took the holy sacrament, Christ Himself appeared with the Holy Grail and held it above Sir Galahad, and blessed him. As the purest of knights knelt in prayer, he heard Christ say, "Come forth, thou servant of Jesus Christ, and thou shalt see that, that hath been thy desire to see."

"Lord, I thank Thee," prayed Sir Galahad, "for now I see that that hath been my desire many a day. Now, blessed Lord, I would not longer live if it might please Thee, Lord."

Suddenly the soul of Sir Galahad departed to be with Jesus

[1]Tennyson, not Malory.

Christ. A great multitude of angels bore his soul up to heaven, for only the pure in heart may see God. Then the Holy Grail was taken up also. No one has ever seen it since.

When King Arthur listened to all the recitals of the knights of his Round Table, none pleased him as much as the quest of Sir Galahad, "whose strength was as the strength of ten because his heart was pure."

THE FIERY FURNACE

Adapted from Daniel III

The early sun's rays blazed down upon the great, golden image on the plain of Dura near the city of Babylon. Standing ninety feet high, about as high as a flagpole, this glimmering image could be seen for miles around. Gathered on the plain was a multitude of richly dressed people — princes and rulers, governors and soldiers — all the mighty men of the empire who had come for the dedication of the image set up by Nebuchadnezzar.

Above the confusion and babble of the people sounded the cry of the heralds of the king, "O people, nations, and languages, when you hear the sound of the cornet, flute, harp, and all kinds of music, fall down and worship the golden image that the king has set up. Whoever falls not down and worships shall be cast the same hour into the midst of a burning fiery furnace!"

While the various instruments poured forth the strains of the music all Babylon loved, the people bowed in worship as the king had commanded. Who wanted to burn in blazing coals?

Were all bowing? Over on the other side of the great image there were one, two, — yes, three men standing upright, not bowing to the image! Did they not hear the herald's cry? Some of the rulers watched them. They saw that they were Shadrach, Meshach, and Abed-nego, the Jewish captives who had refused to drink the king's wine.

Again the trumpets sounded, and the drums were beaten. Still the people continued to kneel down and to worship. But not those three Jews! They worshiped the Lord God only. They remembered His commands: "Thou shalt have no other gods before me. Thou shalt not make unto thee any graven image . . . nor bow down to them . . ." The king's command would not change their decision!

A Babylonian prince edged nearer to the Jewish captives whom Nebuchadnezzar had given such high offices. What a chance to get even with them! Shadrach, Meshach, and Abed-

*Laura S. Emerson, Reprinted from *Spiritual Life Series* (Junior Quarterly; Wesley Press).

nego did not see him. They were looking up to heaven in worship of Jehovah God.

Quickly the jealous prince and his followers hurried to the king. "O King, live for ever! You have made a law that at the sound of the music, every man shall fall down and worship the golden image; whoever does not shall be cast into the midst of a burning fiery furnace. There are certain Jews who have no regard for you nor your gods, and do not worship the golden image you have set up."

Nebuchadnezzar, in rage and fury, red of face, ordered Shadrach, Meshach, and Abed-nego brought before him. Would they dare to put a loyalty to God above their personal safety?

Fearlessly, the three young Jews came and stood before the angry king. They were calm. That made the king more angry. In fairness, he offered them one more chance to hear the music and to bow down to his golden image.

Respectfully, Shadrach, Meshach, and Abed-nego together answered the king, "O Nebuchadnezzar, we are ready to answer you at once. Our God whom we serve is able to deliver us from the burning fiery furnace, and out of your hand, O king. But if it is not God's will to save us, we will not serve your gods, nor worship the golden image that you have set up!"

Such boldness made the king more furious than before. He ordered the furnace heated seven times hotter than it had ever been! Forgetting his former kindness to them, he commanded the soldiers to bind Shadrach, Meshach, and Abed-nego with ropes. They were wearing loose-flowing robes, and turbans on their heads.

Then his mighty men threw them into the roaring furnace. The flames rushed from the furnace with such force that those who cast them in were burned to death! As the three Jewish youths fell down into the midst of the burning fiery furnace, the king sat back satisfied. He'd hear no more of these captives who dared to disobey his law!

But as the raging king looked into the door of the furnace, he began to tremble. "Did we not bind — three men — before casting them — into the fire?"

"True, O king."

"I see four men — loose — walking in the furnace. The fourth — He looks like — like the Son of God!"

Nebuchadnezzar was stunned and afraid. Staggering toward the door of the furnace, he called out, "Shadrach, Meshach, and

Abed-nego, servants of the most high God, come out of the fire and come to me!"

Then Shadrach, Meshach, and Abed-nego came out! They stood before the king and his nobles. Everyone looked at them in amazement! They were alive! Their clothes were not scorched, nor their hair singed! They could not even smell smoke upon them!

"Blessed be the God of Shadrach, Meshach, and Abed-nego, who sent His angel and delivered His servants who trusted in Him and would not worship any god except their own God," cried the king. "I make a law that if anyone in my kingdom shall say a word against their God, he shall be cut in pieces and his house torn down. There is no other God that can deliver like this!"

Then Nebuchadnezzar promoted Shadrach, Meshach, and Abed-nego who had trusted the Lord to deliver them even from a burning fiery furnace.

THE MAID OF EMMAUS*

Agnes Sligh Turnbull

Passover week, and a long hard day at the inn in Emmaus! From early morning Martha had run here and there, carrying water from the spring, bringing sticks, hurrying faster and faster under the sharp commands from old Sarah and the quick blows from Jonas, the husband of Sarah. But this week, in spite of the hard days, Martha had moved as if in a happy dream; for she, too, was planning a pilgrimage.

So, three days before Passover, she was started off on the donkey with the baskets of food and wine hanging from the saddle, on her first trip to Jerusalem. After several frightened inquiries, she had found the street of the Bakers where Anah lived and had given her the food and wine. Then she started off again through the narrow streets, her heart almost bursting with eagerness. She was going to see the Temple!

Within a few rods of it a group of people blocked the way. They had been listening, evidently, to a rabbi and were waiting until He should speak again. Scarcely glancing at them, Martha tried with some impatience to skirt the crowd. Then a voice spoke, and as though it had called her by name, she stopped wonderingly. Over the heads of the people she could hear it:

"A certain man planted a vineyard, and let it forth to husbandmen, and went into a far country."

It seemed to draw her as if a hand had reached out and caught her own. Cautiously she moved around the outer edge of the crowd, coming up at the side quite near to the speaker. Then she saw His face. Tired it looked, and sad, but oh, the infinite tenderness of it! Martha watched it with starving eyes.

Suddenly He turned and saw Martha standing there, one arm about the small donkey's neck. His eyes read hers gravely, then He smiled and held out His hand.

"Thou art little Martha."

And at the gentleness of it she found herself at His feet, sobbing out a wordless tale of the loneliness and weariness of her

*Adapted from *Far above Rubies* by Agnes Sligh Turnbull. (New York: Copyright by Fleming H. Revell Co., 1926). Reprinted by permission.

132

life with old Jonas and Sarah. Then she felt His hand on her head, and a peace and joy indescribable came over her.

"Fear not, little Martha; thou, too, shalt be My disciple."

She raised her eyes.

"Master, what is thy name?"

"I am called Jesus."

"*The Christ*," finished a fair young man, who stood close beside Him.

Then she kissed the blue and white tassels of His robe and came away, forgetting all about the Temple.

The same rocky road; the same harsh Jonas and Sarah at the end of it; the same inn with its hard duties from daylight till dark; but not the same Martha. He, the strange Master, had called her a disciple; His hands had been laid tenderly on her head in blessing.

One thought had gradually risen above all others. She longed to make Him a gift — something to show Him how much she loved Him. At first the idea brought only a sense of helplessness and despair. What had she, Martha of the inn, that she could give? She had lain awake a long time one night, watching the stars and wondering.

Then, as she sat beside the mill in the morning, grinding the wheat and barley, the idea came; she could make Him some little loaves. Oh, not the kind she made for use at the inn, but perfect loaves of the finest of wheat. And she would go again to Jerusalem, as soon as the Passover week was over, and lay them in His hands. She had discovered that over the next hill there lived a man who had a wonderful kind of wheat which made flour as white as snow.

Suddenly she remembered her one possession from the fair past to which her mother belonged — a gold chain, which for some reason Sarah had not taken from her. She loved to feel it and watch the shine of the gold, but it could go for the wheat if the man would accept it.

The next days, strangely enough for Martha, went as she had hoped they would. She had gone, undiscovered, with the gold chain to the man and returned with the fine wheat.

Martha awoke, very early — while it was yet dark. It was the first day of the week. It was her great day. In the twinkling of an eye she had slipped into her clothes, rolled up and put away her pallet, and started her work. She moved softly, taking up and setting down each article with stealthy care. If Jonas or Sarah should waken? The fear was suffocating.

Martha bent over the small, low oven in an agony of hope and fear, then lifted out the loaves with shaking hands. If there should be one mark, one blemish!

But there was not. In the full light of the doorway she realized with a trembling joy, past belief, that they were perfect. All four of them. White as snow, and light and even.

A stirring came from overhead. She caught up the fresh napkin and spread it on the basket. Upon it she laid the little loaves with exquisite care, folded it over them, and then fled out of the inn door and along the street in the direction of the shining light.

When Emmaus was left well behind and she had started up the first long hill she stopped running and drew a long, shuddering breath of relief. She was safely on her way to the Master. Jonas and Sarah could not stop her now. And here in the basket were her gifts of love.

As she walked on, she became aware of a new aliveness in the air about her. Joy gave her strength and lightness of foot. Before she thought it possible, she was entering once more the Joppa gate.

Her plan had been quite simple. She could find the Master, doubtless, near the Temple where He had been before. She would wait with the crowd and listen as long as He taught. Then when the others were all gone, she would go up to Him and give Him the loaves.

She neared the entrance of the Temple and paused uncertainly. One of the chief priests was walking back and forth along the corridors. She went close behind him.

"Hast thou seen Jesus, the Christ?"

The great man started violently. His face was ashy gray. One arm shot threateningly toward her.

"Why askest thou me? Speak not the name to me! Begone!"

Martha trembled with dismay as she ran away from the Temple and down the next street. What could the gentle Master have done to anger the priest so?

She continued her search. Everywhere people hurrying about their duties; here and there groups excitedly talking; but no sign of the rabbi and the young man who had stood beside Him.

Two soldiers passed. She feared them, yet respected their power. Perhaps they could help her. She cautiously touched the arm of the one nearest her.

"Dost thou know where the rabbi Jesus is? They call Him the Christ."

The soldier looked at the other and laughed a strange, mirthless laugh. It pierced Martha's heart with a sense of impending doom.

"Hearest thou that? She asks us if we know aught of Jesus — we who helped crucify Him the other day."

From Martha's bloodless face her great dark eyes met the soldier's agonized. He paused and spoke a little more softly:

"Thou hast the truth, child. He was crucified three days ago on Golgotha Hill. Devils they were who ordered it, but so it fell. Thou hast the truth."

They passed on. Martha leaned, sick and fainting, against the wall. Crucified! Dead! And in her basket were the little loaves for Him. And He would never know. His hands would never touch them. The gentle Master, with only love and pity in His face — crucified! And the loaves were white as snow — perfect — to show her love for Him.

The afternoon sun was hot now, and Martha's feet were heavy. The deep dust of the road rose to choke and blind her. The sharp stones tripped her and cut her feet. The way back was endless, for now there was no hope. She thought wearily of the freshness and joy of the morning. There would never be such beauty and happiness for her again. She stumbled on — and on.

When she reached the inn, at last, it was late afternoon. She was about to enter the main door when she caught her breath. No, she could not surrender the basket to Jonas and Sarah. Better to crush the little loaves in her hands and allow the birds of the air to have them.

She set the basket down beside the eastern door — Sarah rarely went out that way — then went to the front of the inn. With a shout they were both upon her.

The blows came, as she had known they would. She had no strength to resist. She lay where she had fallen, beside the oven — the oven where only at daybreak she had labored in ecstasy.

Martha lay still. Soon, darkness; but not as of last night filled with angels. Dead, despairing, empty darkness, tonight. She closed her eyes.

All at once there were footsteps along the street. Voices were talking earnestly. She recognized one of them. It was that of Cleopas, the rich vineyard owner. He always stopped at the inn on his trips, to and from Jerusalem. A hand opened the door.

"Abide with us," she heard Cleopas say eagerly, "for the day is far spent."

Then they entered: Cleopas and his brother Simon, and another, — a stranger whose face was in the shadow.

Martha had risen with infinite pain and now set about placing the food upon the table. She brought the barley cakes and oil, and wine and raisins, and the meal was ready. Then she stopped. Just outside the eastern door was the basket with its precious offering — the gift of love that couldn't be bestowed. Here were three men, weary from their journey and hungry.

The struggle in her breast was bitter but it was brief. She opened the door and lifted the basket. From their napkin she took the four loaves and placed them before the stranger, who sat in the shadow at the head of the table. Her eyes, dim with tears, watched the loaves as they lay there, snowy and fair. The longing love of her heart; the gold chain, her one treasure; her aching limbs; the swelling bruises on her poor beaten body; all these had helped to purchase them. She raised her eyes to the stranger's face — then, a cry!

It was as though all the color of the sunset and the radiance of the morning had united behind it.

And out from the shining, majestic and glorified, yet yearning in its compassion and love, *The Face,* but not that of a stranger, appeared.

He was gazing steadfastly upon the little loaves. He touched them, broke them, extended them, and raised His eyes to heaven, while the blinding glory increased.

Cleopas and Simon were leaning forward, breathless, transfixed. Martha had crept closer and knelt within the circle of light.

"Master," she tried to whisper. "Master!"

He turned and looked upon her. No need to speak that which was upon her heart. He knew. He understood.

Gently the radiance enfolded her. Upon her shone the beneficent smile, frought with the heavenly benediction and healing for all earth's wounds.

Then, as softly as the sunset had shone, the celestial light died away. The Master's chair was empty.

Cleopas and Simon sat spellbound, gazing at the place where the splendor had been. Martha still knelt in a rapture of joy and peace.

On the table lay the little white loaves, uneaten, but received and blessed.

THE BOY HANDEL*

Laura S. Emerson

Who sang the first Christmas song? That's right — the angels over the plains of Bethlehem. Do you remember the chorus? "Glory to God in the highest, and peace on earth, good will towards men."

Those beautiful words were taken from the Scriptures, but it was a great musician who composed the stately music which thousands of choirs sing every Christmas.

Little George loved melody. He liked to listen to the murmur of the brook, the clot, clot of the horses' trot, and best of all, the songs of the birds in his native German village nearly three centuries ago. Over and over again in his mind, he hummed the beautiful songs he heard at work and play. The happiest time of the day was at the end of the long afternoon when his school-master sat at his spinet, an instrument like a small piano, and played simple tunes for his boys. George would stand close by and watch his teacher's fingers race over the keys.

"If only I had a spinet, I know I could learn to play on it myself," he sighed.

But George's doctor-father didn't want his son to waste his life with music. He wanted him to be a lawyer, so he wouldn't let anyone teach George even the scale.

One day a kind member of his family smuggled a spinet up the long stairs to a far corner of the attic. Then carefully each string was wound with strips of cloth, so that when it was played not a tinkle could be heard in the rooms below.

After his studies were over and the rest of the household was in bed, little George would tiptoe up to the dark attic, put his short fingers on the keys, and pick out the melody that had been ringing in his head all day.

One night George so completely lost himself in his music that he used the swell at its greatest volume, flooding the attic with joyous tones. Faint sounds crept down through the floor, soft and weird, as if the house were haunted. The whole family was

*Reprinted from *Trailblazer,* Copyright 1953, by W. L. Jenkins. Used by permission.

awakened. Lighting a lantern, his father led the search. Finally he opened the low attic door and flashed his lantern around. There was his small son in his night clothes and cap, playing on a musical intrument!

"George!" he called out sternly.

The melodies stopped suddenly.

"Music will do you no good. You are to be a lawyer," vowed his father. When he saw his boy, whom he loved, trembling before him, he relented. "You may keep the instrument, but don't disturb the household again!"

Then how happy George Frederick Handel was! The English artist, Margaret Dicksee, has painted this picture for us.

One morning, George, who was seven now, learned that his father was going to visit the Duke of Saxe-Weissenfels. There would be beautiful music at the royal court, he knew.

"Please take me to the palace with you," he begged.

"Another time," he answered, for the coach was at the door.

George watched sadly as the horses' hoofs clattered over the rough cobblestones. It was a long, forty-mile journey to the court of the duke.

Suddenly George's face brightened. He started running after the carriage as fast as his short legs would carry him. On and on he followed through the hot sun, over the dusty, rocky road. Finally the jolting coach stopped and George cried out, "Father, wait!"

Dr. Handel peered down the road and saw his weary little boy. What should he do? He had gone too far to send him back. Telling him how naughty he had been, he took him up on the seat beside him where George soon fell fast asleep.

Next morning, George watched the organist play the great chapel organ. Seeing his great delight, the organist in fun invited George to play. The seven-year-old musician filled him with amazement. On Sunday, the organist let him play part of the solemn service. When the duke saw a child at his organ, he asked who he was.

"Little Handel from Halle," was the reply that was brought to him.

Then the duke was pleased and called George to him and learned about his secret practice and how he had taught himself to play on his spinet. When the duke found that George's father didn't encourage his talent, he interceded for him and commanded his father to give him the best musical training possible.

So the little boy who loved music studied diligently, composing his own pieces. Soon he mastered the organ and the violin, and began directing orchestras. Later he went to London where he wrote his great oratorio, *The Messiah*, with the angels' song we all like to sing at Christmastide.

BETTY'S RIDE*

Henry Seidel Canby

The sun was just rising and showering his first rays on the roof and solid walls of a house surrounded by a grove of walnut trees and overlooking one of the valleys so common in south-eastern Pennsylvania. When Ezra Dale had become the leader of the little band of Quakers which gathered here every First Day, he had built the house under the walnut trees and had taken his wife, Ann, and his little daughter, Betty, to live there.

The sun rose higher, and just as its beams touched the broad stone step in front of the house, the door opened, and Ann Dale, a sweet-faced woman in the plain Quaker dress came out, followed by Betty, a little blue-eyed Quakeress of twelve years with a gleam of spirit in her face.

"Betty," said her mother, as they walked out toward the great horse block by the roadside, "thee must keep house today. Friend Robert has just sent thy father word that the redcoats have not crossed the Brandywine since the Third Day last, and thy father and I will ride to Chester today, that there may be other than corncakes and bacon for the friends who come to us after monthly meeting. Mind thee keeps near the house and finishes thy sampler."

"Yes, Mother," said Betty, "but thee will not come early. I shall miss thee sadly."

Just then Ezra appeared, wearing his collarless Quaker coat, and leading a horse saddled with a great pillion, into which Ann climbed after her husband. With a final warning and "fare-well" to Betty, Ann clasped him tightly round the waist lest she should be jolted off as they jogged down the rough and winding lane into the Chester road.

Friend Ann had many reasons for fearing to leave Betty alone for a whole day, and she looked back anxiously at her waving "farewell" with her little bonnet.

It was a troublous time. The Revolution was at its height, and the British, who had a short time before disembarked their

*Reprinted from *Childcraft*. Copyright by Henry Seidel Canby. Used by permission.

army near Elkton, Maryland, were now encamped near White Clay Creek, while Washington occupied the country bordering the Brandywine. His army was small and bands of the British sometimes crossed the Brandywine and foraged the fertile counties of Delaware and Chester. As Betty's father was known to be a patriot, he had to suffer the fortunes of war with his neighbors.

Thus with many anxious thoughts, Betty's mother watched the slight figure under the spreading branches of a great chestnut tree, which seemed to rustle its unnumerable leaves as if to protect the little maid. However, the sun shone brightly, the swallows chirped as they circled overhead, and nothing seemed farther off than the war.

Betty skipped merrily into the house and, snatching up some broken corncake left from the morning meal, ran lightly out to the pasture where Daisy was kept, her own horse, which she had helped to raise from a colt.

"Come here, Daisy," she said, as she seated herself on the top rail of the fence. "Come here, and thee shall have some of thy mistress' corncake. Ah! I thought thee would like it. Now go and eat all thee can of this good grass, for if the wicked redcoats come again, thee will not have another chance, I can tell thee."

Daisy whinnied and trotted off, while Betty, after feeding the few chickens, returned up to the house, and getting her sampler, sat down under a walnut tree to sew.

All was quiet except the chattering of the squirrels overhead and the drowsy hum of the bees, when from around the curve in the road she heard a shot, then another nearer, and then a voice shouting commands, and then the thud of hoofbeats farther down the valley. She jumped up with a startled cry, "The redcoats! The redcoats! Oh, what shall I do!"

Just then the first of the soldiers, their buff and blue uniforms showing them to be Americans, appeared in full flight around the curve in the road and, springing over the fence, dashed across the pasture straight for the meeting-house. Through the broad gateway they poured, and forcing open the door of the meeting-house, rushed within and began to bar the windows.

Their leader paused while his men passed in; seeing Betty, he came quickly toward her.

"What do you here, child?" he said, hurriedly. "Go quickly, before the British reach us, and tell your father that he shall ride to Washington, on the Brandywine, and tell him that we, only one hundred men, are besieged by three hundred British cavalry in Chester meeting-house, with but little powder left. Tell him to make all haste to us."

Turning, he ran into the meeting-house, now made into a fort, and as the doors closed behind him, Betty saw a black gun pointing from every window.

With trembling fingers the little maid picked up her sampler, and as the horses' hoofs grew louder, she ran into the house, locked and bolted the heavy door, and then ran up the broad stairs and seated herself in a little window overlooking the meeting-house yard. She had gone into the house none too soon. Up the road, with their redcoats gleaming, swept the British cavalry, never stopping until they reached the meeting-house — and then it was too late.

A sheet of flame shot out from the wall before them, and half a dozen troopers fell to the ground, and half a dozen horses, without their riders, galloped down the road. The leader shouted a sharp command, and the whole troop retreated in confusion.

Betty drew back shuddering, and when she looked again the troopers had got off their horses, surrounded the meeting-house, and were pouring volley after volley at its doors and windows. Then for the first time Betty thought of the officer's message, and remembered that the safety of the Americans depended upon her, for her father was away, no neighbor within reach, and without powder she knew they could not resist long.

Could she save them? Stealing softly into the pasture behind the barn, she saddled Daisy and led her through the bars into the wood road, which opened into the highway just around the bend. Could she but pass the pickets without their seeing her, there would be little danger of pursuit; then there would be only the long ride of eight miles ahead of her.

Just before the narrow road joined the broader highway, Betty mounted Daisy, and starting off at a gallop, she had just turned the corner when a voice shouted, "Halt!" and a shot whistled past her head. Betty screamed with terror, and bending over, brought down her riding whip with all her strength upon Daisy, then, turning for a moment, saw three troopers hurriedly mounting.

Her heart sank within her, but, beginning to feel the excitement of the chase, she leaned over and patted Daisy on the neck, begging her to do her best. Onward they sped.

But Daisy had not been used for weeks and already felt the unusual strain. Now they thundered over Naaman's Creek, now over Concord, with the nearest trooper only four hundred yards behind. Now they raced beside the clear waters of Beaver

Brook, and as Betty dashed through its shallow ford, the sound of horses' hoofs seemed just over her shoulder.

Betty, at first sure of success, now knew that unless in some way she could throw her pursuers off her track she was surely lost. Just then she saw ahead of her a fork in the road, the lower branch leading to the Brandywine, the upper to Birmingham meeting-house. If she could get the troopers on the upper road while she took the lower, she would be safe. As if in answer to her wish, she remembered the old crossroad which, long disused and with its entrance hidden by drooping boughs, led from a point in the upper road just out of sight of the fork down across the lower, and through the valley of the Brandywine. Could she gain this road unseen, she still might reach Washington.

She urged Daisy forward, and just in time broke through the dense growth which hid the entrance, and sat trembling, hidden behind a dense growth of tangled vines, while she heard the troopers ride by. Then, riding through the woods, she came at last into the open, and saw beneath her the beautiful valley of the Brandywine, with the white tents of the American army.

She started off at a gallop and dashed around a bend in the road into the midst of a group of officers riding slowly up from the valley.

"Stop, little maiden, before you run us down," said one, who seemed to be in command. "Where are you going in such a hurry?"

"Oh, sir," said Betty, "can thee tell me where I can find General Washington?"

"Yes, little Quakeress," said the officer who had first spoken to her, "I am General Washington. What do you wish?"

Betty poured forth her story in a few broken sentences, fell forward in her saddle, and for the first time in her life fainted, worn out by her exciting ride. But she had saved the Americans in the Quaker meeting-house.

When Betty recovered from the shock of her long ride and awoke from a deep sleep, she found her mother kneeling beside her little bed, while her father talked with General Washington himself beside the fireplace. It was the proudest moment of her life when Washington came forward and took her by the hand and said,

"You are the bravest little maid in America, and an honor to your country."

A LESSON OF FAITH*

Julia Darrow Cowles

A mild, green Caterpillar was one day strolling about on a cabbage leaf, when there settled beside her a beautiful Butterfly. The Butterfly fluttered her wings feebly and seemed very ill.

"I feel very strange and dizzy," said the Butterfly, addressing the Caterpillar, "and I am sure that I have but a little while to live. But I have just laid some butterfly eggs on this cabbage leaf, and if I die there will be no one to care for my baby butterflies. I must hire a nurse for them at once, but I cannot go far to seek for one. May I hire you as nurse, kind Caterpillar? I will pay you with gold dust from my wings."

Then, before the surprised Caterpillar could reply, the Butterfly went on, "Of course, you must not feed them on the coarse cabbage leaves which are your food. Young butterflies must be fed upon early dew and the honey of flowers. And at first, oh, good Caterpillar, they must not be allowed to fly far, for their wings will not be strong. It is sad that you cannot fly yourself. But I am sure you will be kind and will do the best you can."

With that the poor Butterfly drooped her wings and died, and the Caterpillar had no chance to so much as say "Yes," or "No."

"Dear me!' she exclaimed, as she looked at the butterfly eggs beside her, "What sort of a nurse will I make for a group of gay young butterflies? Much attention they will pay to the advice of a plain caterpillar like me. But I shall have to do the best that I can," she added. And all that night she walked around and around the butterfly eggs to see that no harm came to them.

"I wish that I had someone wiser than myself to consult," she said to herself next morning. "I might talk it over with the house dog. But, no," she added hastily, "he is kind, but big and rough, and one brush of his tail would whisk all the eggs off the cabbage leaf."

"There is Tom Cat," she went on, after thinking a few

*Adapted for telling. By permission of the publishers. Reprinted from *The Art of Storytelling*.

moments, "but he is lazy and selfish, and he would not give himself the trouble to think about butterfly eggs.

"Ah, but there's the Lark!" she exclaimed at length. "He flies far up into the heavens and perhaps he knows more than we creatures that live upon the earth. I'll ask him."

So the Caterpillar sent a message to the Lark, who lived in a neighboring cornfield, and she told him all her troubles.

"And I want to know how I, a poor crawling Caterpillar, am to feed and care for a family of beautiful young butterflies. Could you find out for me the next time you fly away up into the blue heavens?"

"Perhaps I can," said the Lark, and off he flew.

Higher and higher he winged his way until the poor, crawling Caterpillar could not even hear his song, to say nothing of seeing him.

After a very long time — at least it seemed so to the Caterpillar, who, in her odd, lumbering way, kept walking around and around the butterfly eggs — the Lark came back.

First, she could hear his song away up in the heavens. Then it sounded nearer and nearer, till he alighted close beside her and began to speak.

"I found out many wonderful things," he said. "But if I tell them to you, you will not believe me."

"Oh, yes I will," answered the Caterpillar hastily, "I believe everything I am told."

"Well, then," said the Lark, "the first thing I found out was that the butterfly eggs will turn into little green caterpillars, just like yourself, and that they will eat cabbage leaves just as you do."

"Wretch!" exclaimed the Caterpillar, bristling with indignation. "Why do you come and mock me with such a story as that? I thought you would be kind and would try to help me."

"So I would," answered the Lark, "but I told you, you would not believe me," and with that he flew away to the cornfield.

"Dear me," said the Caterpillar, sorrowfully. "When the Lark flies so far up into the heavens I should not think he would come back to us poor creatures with such a silly tale. And I needed help so badly."

"I would help you if you would only believe me," said the Lark, flying down to the cabbage patch once more. "I have wonderful things to tell you, if you would only have faith in me and trust in what I say."

"And you are not making fun of me?" asked the Caterpillar.

"Of course not," answered the Lark.

"But you tell me such impossible things!"

"If you could fly with me and see the wonders that I see, here on earth and away up in the blue sky, you would not say that *anything* was *impossible*," replied the Lark.

"But," said the Caterpillar, "you tell me that these eggs will hatch out into caterpillars, and I *know* that their mother was a butterfly, for I saw her with my own eyes; and so, of course, they will be butterflies. How could they be anything else? I am sure I can reason that far, even if I cannot fly."

"Very well," answered the Lark, "then I must leave you, though I have even more wonderful things that I could tell. But what comes to you from the heavens, you can only receive by faith, as I do. You cannot crawl around on your cabbage leaf and reason these things out."

"Oh, I do believe what I am told," repeated the Caterpillar — although she had just proved that it was not true — "at least," she added, "everything that is *reasonable* to believe. Pray tell me what else you learned."

"I learned," said the Lark, impressively, "that you will be a butterfly, yourself, some day."

"Now, indeed, you are making fun of me," exclaimed the Caterpillar, ready to cry with vexation and disappointment. But just at that moment she felt something brush against her side, and, turning her head, she looked in amazement at the cabbage leaf, for there, just coming out of the butterfly eggs, were eight or ten little green caterpillars — and they were no more than out of the eggs before they began eating the juicy leaf.

Oh, how astonished and how ashamed the Caterpillar felt. What the Lark had said was true!

And then a very wonderful thought came to the poor, green Caterpillar. "If this part is true, it must all be true, and some day *I* shall be a *butterfly*."

She was so delighted that she began telling all her caterpillar friends about it — but they did not believe her any more than she had believed the Lark.

"But I know, I *know*," she kept saying to herself. And she never tired of hearing the Lark sing of the wonders of the earth below, and of the heavens above.

And all the time, the little green caterpillars on the leaf grew and thrived wonderfully, and the big green Caterpillar watched them and cared for them carefully every hour.

One day the Caterpillar's friends gathered around her and said, very sorrowfully, "It is time for you to spin your chrysalis and die."

But the Caterpillar replied, "You mean that I shall soon be changed into a beautiful butterfly. How wonderful it will be."

And her friends looked at one another sadly and said, "She is quite out of her mind."

Then the Caterpillar spun her chrysalis and went to sleep.

And by and by, when she awakened, oh, then she *knew* that what the Lark had learned in the heavens was true — for she was a beautiful butterfly, with gold dust on her wings.

LITTLE HECTOR HELICOPTER*

A Read-Aloud Story in Rhyme

Georgia Tucker Smith

Little Hector Helicopter stood beside the hangar door. He blinked his eyes; he'd never been out in the sun before. Other helicopters and planes were everywhere — some taking off, some landing, some high up in the air.

His mother stood beside him. "You're going to fly today; you're going to carry mail to towns not very far away."

"Carry mail!" cried Hector. "Why, that's no fun at all. Why can't I do exciting things? Because I am so small? I wish I were an aeroplane, so I could fly real high — so high I couldn't see the ground, just fluffy clouds and sky. Watch that blue plane loop the loop. He did a tail spin, too." Hector sighed. "A head spin is all that I can do. If I tried a tail spin, I'd land PLUNK, upside down. My rotor paddles would spank me" he added with a frown.

"You'll carry gifts and letters, dear." His mother shook her head. "Think about the happiness that you will bring," she said.

"But I won't see their happiness," said Hector. "When I land, I want a crowd to meet me — sometimes, perhaps, a band."

"It's time to go," his mother said. "Now do the best you can." Hector's rotor whirled and swished like an electric fan. Little bugs clung to the grass, caught in the sudden breeze; birds, chirping loudly, flapped their wings and left the swaying trees. Up, up he went! "Good-by," he called above the whirring noise. Soon, houses, cows, and horses looked like pretty little toys. He saw a river, then a town! His fan went slower, slower as he neared the little town; then he went lower, lower.

Town after town he visited and left big sacks of mail right on time, right on the spot, exactly, without fail. Hector wasn't even tired when he got home that night; he smiled and told his mother about his pleasant flight.

"Rest awhile," his mother said. "A square dance soon will start right here on our landing field, and you must do your part."

*Reprinted from *Wee Wisdom* and used by permission of the author.

"A square dance!" Hector whirled about. "I can't dance, but I'll try. I can follow orders. Don't worry; I'll get by."

"The planes can't dance," his mother said. "Their wings take too much space; only helicopters have the swing and poise and grace."

Hector smiled. "I'll be right there!" He wasn't even late. He swung around the corner like swinging on a gate; he promenaded right and left; he bowed and do-sedoed. He gayly danced each dance in turn, so happy that he glowed.

A few days later the sky was gray, and Hector's way was dim; the clouds he wished to fly above had not come down to him. It rained and rained. The river rose! Hector blinked his eyes and looked down on the swollen stream in wonder and surprise. In the raging torrent, its wild waves leaping high, Hector saw a barn, a fence, and then a house swirl by.

He looked again, and on the roof he saw a boy and girl. With arms upstretched, they called to him. He gave his fan a whirl, and down he went real close so he could get a better view. He thought, "Now this is something that no plane could ever do." Hector stopped, still in the air; the pilot dropped a rope; the children's faces seemed to glow with thankfulness and hope. The girl came first, and then the boy. When they were safe inside, Hector whirled his rotor fan with happiness and pride. And when they'd crossed the river and reached the little town, he paused; then slowly, carefully, he brought the children down.

He thought, "It isn't size that counts; it isn't speed or style; it isn't waiting crowds and bands—it's doing things worth while." Then he thought, as up he whirled above a field of clover, "Just knowing you are needed makes you feel good all over."

THE SHINING SECRET*

Helen Frazee Bower

Late one Sunday afternoon, just before Christmas, Mrs. Gordon and her two children entered the living room of their home. It was almost dusk and the Christmas tree seemed to blaze brighter than ever in the corner of the room. They all stood very quietly — awed almost — watching it.

"We've never had such a beautiful tree, Mother," said Peter, "and I think it's the new star at the top that makes it extra beautiful."

"Just like a shining secret up there," murmured Margaret.

"Christmas is a shining secret," replied Mother with a smile.

"What do you mean by that?" they asked in unison.

"Well, this is our story hour and I'll tell you all about it," said Mother as she seated herself in the big armchair. She turned it so that she and the young people at her feet could sit facing the tree, with its brilliant star beaming upon them, and began:

"In the long and long ago, at the time of creation, 'when the morning stars sang together, and all the sons of God shouted for joy,' there was one little star to whom God spoke. It had always been an ordinary star — no different from the rest — going on about its business of shining, not knowing that it had any special dignity or importance.

"That Is, It Was That Way until God Spoke.

"One morning, out of the silence of eternity, God leaned into space and time and whispered to the little star a shining secret. Then, with the secret in its heart, the little star glowed, and glowed. Its face became more bright and shining than ever before. It shown right out of its ordinary self into something special and glorious. It was no longer just another little star. It had become the Star of the Ages.

"On it shone — past all the pleasant places of heaven, on down through the thick clouds of human trouble, through wars and rumors of wars, through heartbreak and disaster, beyond sin and its consequences. The shining star traversed the years, blazing

*Reprinted from the *King's Business* and used by permission of the author.

150

a path of splendor right down into this dark world of ours, until it came to rest at last above a barn in Bethlehem.

"At first, this was a very ordinary little barn — just a hole in the wall, really — not spacious and noble-looking at all, in fact, not nearly so fine as some of its neighbors.

"That Is, It Was That Way until God Spoke.

"One morning, out of the silence of eternity, God leaned into space and time and whispered to the little barn a shining secret. With the secret in its heart, it grew, and it grew, and it grew, though the outward measurements of it did not change. It grew until it filled all the world with its importance. It was no longer an ordinary little barn. It had become the Barn of the Ages. No other place in all the world knew what it knew.

"The barn was so full of the shining secret that it could hardly stay in its hole in the wall. It could scarcely keep still and wait. All around, it saw 'men's hearts failing them for fear'; it saw pain and pride, sin and sorrow, and sometimes it wanted to cry out, 'If you only knew what I know!'

"But it did not cry out, for God had said it was to sit by a road in Bethlehem and wait. God is like that, you know. He sends a star on a long, long journey through the years to tell a shining secret; but He says to a barn in Bethlehem, 'Be still and know.'

"Always some must go, and some must wait. It is the way of the world, and it is God's way, too. It is a good way.

"So the barn waited, and waited, and waited — until, 'in the fulness of time,' it looked up one night into the sky that was full of ordinary stars, and there was *the* star, glowing with a very special and radiant wonder.

"The star winked and said, 'I know a secret,' and the barn blinked its single eye of light that was one tiny window, and said, 'I know it, too'; and they smiled happily at each other. There, in the darkness they waited together in that quietness of long ago.

"They were waiting for a *woman.* For, not many miles away, in the village of Nazareth, God had spoken to someone. She was just an ordinary woman — no one of high degree or great achievement, not very different from other women of her time, except that she was very good and sweet and kind — just a girl, really, an ordinary girl with a gentle, loving heart.

"That Is, It Was That Way Until God Spoke to Her.

"One morning, out of the silence of eternity, God leaned into space and time, and sent His angel, Gabriel, to whisper to the woman a shining secret. The woman pondered the secret in her heart, and was so filled with the wonder of it that it overflowed into the shining depths of her eyes. She was still an ordinary woman — not better than others, not divine — needing, as every member of our sinning race needs, a Saviour to atone for sin. But now, this ordinary woman was consumed by a shining secret, a secret that set her apart, in a sense, as the Woman of the Ages. She went about singing to herself:

> My soul doth magnify the Lord,
> And my spirit hath rejoiced in God my Saviour.
> For he hath regarded the low estate of his handmaiden: . . .
> For he that is mighty hath done to me great things;
> And holy is his name.
> And his mercy is on them that fear him from generation to
> generation.
> My soul doth magnify the Lord.
> And my spirit hath rejoiced in God my Saviour.

"As she sang, she looked down a road — just an ordinary little road — that led to Bethlehem. But it was not an ordinary little road to *her*, for at its end she knew the shining secret waited.

"And suddenly there was the star, spilling a path of radiance across her face, and saying, 'I, too, know it, I have known it a long, long time.'

"They smiled at each other in the darkness — the woman and the star — as she approached an inn.

"As Mary looked at the crowded inn, she could not feel as though her journey was quite complete. But then she saw the little barn, blinking a friendly eye at her, and the bright star waiting above it, and she knew that she was there.

"These three who knew the secret were together now — the star, the barn, and the woman — and there was nothing to wait for any longer. Now it could be told: the thing for which the star had journeyed, for which the barn had waited, and about which the woman had been singing. The shining secret was about to be revealed to the world.

"This was the moment for which earth had waited, and yet it was just an ordinary moment — no different from all the other moments ticked off by time.

"*That Is, It Was This Way until God Spoke.*

"Then it became the Moment of the Ages. For, in the stillness of that first Christmas night, out of the silence of eternity, God leaned into space and time and spoke. And the Word which He spoke was a Babe placed in the arms of the woman. The barn spread its sheltering roof above, and the star looked down through the night with pride and joy.

"It did not matter to the star that it would never shine so brightly again, for it knew that down in the barn lay the Light of the world, beside which all other lights must pale; and it was content. It had had its shining hour, and it never could be really ordinary again.

"The barn knew, too, that one day it would fall into decay, but it did not care, either. For one breathless moment it had cradled infinity, and that was enough. It never could go back to being just the same ordinary place again.

"The woman knew that in the years to come she would recede into the background, and be more or less forgotten as her first-born child, Jesus, Son of God, entered upon His divine mission and went about His Father's business. But she did not complain. She had carried a shining secret in her heart, close to where the little Son of God had slept, and no one could take *that* from her. She never could go back to being just an ordinary woman again."

The story had ended, and the three sat very still.

"And so," Mother finished, "Christmas really is a shining secret, isn't it?"

Out of the darkness, Margaret spoke: "What did God really whisper to the star, and to the barn, and to the woman, Mother? I would like to know."

"I was hoping you would ask me that," said Mother, "for you see it is a shining secret which has never been quite completed. It is being whispered to us, today. I think that what God said to the star, and to the barn, and to the woman was simply this: 'Jesus is coming!' And the shining beauty of that secret was enough to change dull, ordinary things and fill them with wonder and glory."

"Why, how nice!" said Peter. "Then *we* have a secret, too, for Jesus is coming again."

"That's just it," said Mother in a pleased voice. "We have a secret that has power to change the world, to shine out across the dark pages of earth's history, and turn man's heartbreak to rejoicing — a secret that touches ordinary things and ordinary people and fills them with glorious importance. Jesus is coming, and everything is going to be all right."

A HANDFUL OF CLAY*

Henry Van Dyke

There was a handful of clay in the bank of a river. It was only common clay, coarse and heavy; but it had high thoughts of its own value, and wonderful dreams of the great place which it was to fill in the world when the time came for its virtues to be discovered.

Overhead, in the spring sunshine, the trees whispered together of the glory which descended upon them when the delicate blossoms and leaves began to expand; and the forest flowed with fair, clear colors, as if the dust of thousands of rubies and emeralds was hanging, in soft clouds, above the earth.

The flowers, surprised with the joy of beauty, bent their heads to one another, as the wind caressed them and said: "Sisters, how lovely you have become. You make the day bright."

The river, glad of new strength and rejoicing in the unison of all its waters, murmured to the shores in music, telling of its release from icy fetters, its swift flight from the snow-clad mountains, and the mighty work to which it was hurrying — the wheels of many mills to be turned, and great ships to be floated to the sea.

Waiting blindly in its bed, the clay comforted itself with lofty hopes. "My time will come," it said. "I was not made to be hidden forever. Glory and beauty and honor are coming to me in due season."

One day the clay felt itself taken from the place where it had waited so long. A flat blade of iron passed beneath it and lifted it, and tossed it into a cart with other lumps of clay; and it was carried far away, as it seemed, over a rough and stony road. But it was not afraid, nor discouraged, for it said to itself: "This is necessary. The path to glory is always rugged. Now I am on my way to play a great part in the world."

But the hard journey was nothing compared with the tribulation and distress that came after it. The clay was put into a trough and mixed and beaten and stirred and trampled. It

*Reprinted from *The Blue Flower* by Henry Van Dyke. Used by permission of Grosset & Dunlap, Inc., Publishers.

seemed almost unbearable. But there was consolation in the thought that something very fine and noble was certainly coming out of all this trouble. The clay felt sure that, if it could only wait long enough, a wonderful reward was in store for it.

Then it was put upon a swiftly turning wheel, and whirled around until it seemed as if it must fly into a thousand pieces. A strange power pressed it and moulded it as it revolved, and through all the dizziness and pain it felt that it was taking a new form.

Then an unknown hand put it into an oven, and fires were kindled about it — fierce and penetrating — hotter than all the heats of summer that had ever brooded upon the bank of the river. But through all, the clay held itself together and endured the trials, in the confidence of a great future. "Surely," it thought, "I am intended for something very splendid, since such pains are taken with me. Perhaps I am fashioned for the ornament of a temple, or a precious vase for the table of a king."

At last the baking was finished. The clay was taken from the furnace and set down upon a board, in the cool air under the blue sky. The tribulation was passed. The reward was at hand.

Close beside the board there was a pool of water, not very deep, nor very clear, but calm enough to reflect, with impartial truth, every image that fell upon it. There, for the first time, as it was lifted from the board, the clay saw its new shape, the reward of all its patience and pain, the consummation of its hopes — a common flower-pot, straight and stiff, red and ugly. And then it felt that it was not destined for a king's house, nor a palace of art, because it was made without glory or beauty or honor; and it murmured against the unknown maker, saying, "Why hast thou made me thus?"

Many days it passed in sullen discontent. Then it was filled with earth, and something — it knew not what — but something rough and brown and dead-looking was thrust into the middle of the earth and covered over. The clay rebelled at this new disgrace. "This is the worst of all that has happened to me, to be filled with dirt and rubbish. Surely I am a failure."

But presently it was set in a greenhouse, where the sunlight fell warm upon it, and water sprinkled over it, and day by day as it waited, a change began to come to it. Something was stirring within it — a new hope. Still it was ignorant and knew not what the new hope meant.

One day the clay was lifted again from its place, and carried into a great church. Its dream was coming true after all. It had a fine part to play in the world. Glorious music flowed over it. It was surrounded with flowers. Still it could not understand. So it whispered to another vessel of clay, like itself, close beside it, "Why have they set me here? Why do all the people look toward us?" And the other vessel answered, "Do you not know? You are carrying a royal sceptre of lilies. Their petals are white as snow and the heart of them is like pure gold. The people look this way because the flower is the most wonderful in the world. And the root of it is in your heart."

Then the clay was content, and silently thanked its maker, because, though an earthen vessel, it held so great a treasure.

THE WATCH THAT DISAPPEARED*

Artie E. Appleton and Edith Warner

"It's lost! Oh dear, my new watch!" Patty wailed. "It's gone."

"Why, Patty!" Martha exclaimed. "What do you mean? Didn't you lay it over on the window sill while you washed your hands?"

"Of course, I did." Patty was crying now. "Just a minute ago. Oh dear, I just got it for my birthday last week. I've wanted a watch for ever so long, and now it is gone."

"But, Patty, it can't be," Martha tried to reassure her. "It must be here someplace. We will all help you look."

"Yes," Jean chimed in, "it has probably just slipped down behind something."

Five of the girls from the fifth grade were in the school washroom, getting cleaned up for the one o'clock class. But search as hard as they could, there was no watch.

"Someone must have taken it," Patty said firmly. "Several other girls left just a while ago, and I think I know who took it."

"Patty, you don't mean —" Martha hesitated, but she saw by the look in their eyes that the same thought was taking shape in the minds of the others. None of the five girls, who had all started school together, would ever do such a thing. But what about Carla, the strange new girl who had entered their class just last week? Nobody knew a thing about her, except that she was not dressed quite so well as the others and she kept to herself during recess and noon.

The five girls were sober as they took their seats in Miss Bear's room at the ringing of the one o'clock bell. Instinctively their eyes glanced across the room at Carla, and then met one another's with startled looks. Carla was wearing a new watch! From where they sat it was quite impossible to see if it was exactly like Patty's, but it did seem to be.

Miss Bear must have wondered why five of her best pupils lagged so far behind in their work that afternoon. Not one could settle down to spelling and arithmetic.

When the recess bell released them from class, the five girls gathered in a little group around the slide.

*Reprinted from *Wee Wisdom* and used by permission of the authors.

"Didn't I tell you!" Patty exclaimed triumphantly. "It is just as I thought. I am going right now and demand that she return my watch."

"But, Patty, you can't do that," Martha cautioned. "Not until you are sure."

"Well, what do you suggest?"

"We might just go and admire it and ask her when she got it," Jean suggested. "Nobody besides us knows that Patty has lost her watch, and we don't have to warn Carla."

"Well, her story had better be good," Patty said. "The idea of her having nerve enough to put it right on and wear it!"

"Hush, Patty," Martha said. "Let's wait until we find out for sure. It would be awful to accuse Carla of stealing it if she didn't."

"Everybody knows she doesn't have money for watches like that," Patty insisted.

The five girls strolled as casually as they could in Carla's direction. Her face lit up with a happy smile when she saw them coming. They had never paid any attention to her before.

"I see you have a new watch. May we see it?" Jean broke the ice.

Carla extended her arm. Five pairs of eyebrows lifted in surprise. Shock was written on four girlish faces, but Patty's face wore an I-told-you-so expression. The watch was either hers or an exact duplicate.

"I lost a watch just like this one at noon." Patty's voice was grim. "I laid it on the window sill while I washed my hands, and when I went to get it, it was gone."

Carla's narrow face flushed a bright red. "I didn't take it," she stammered. "This is my watch. My — my grandmother sent it to me for my birthday."

"It seems funny you have never worn it before today," Patty snapped.

"But I just got it this noon when I went home for lunch. It came in the morning mail." Carla started to cry, looking helplessly at the five doubting faces that closed around her in an unfriendly circle.

"That will do to tell," Patty scoffed. "As for me, I'm going to report it to Miss Bear immediately. I know that is my watch and I'm going to get it back before I go home from school."

She ran off to the door of the school, jerked it open, and disappeared inside. Martha started to follow but changed her mind. The others slowly drifted away, leaving Carla standing alone, still crying.

"Miss Bear!" Patty burst into the room, her breath coming in short gasps from hurrying and from anger. "Miss Bear, Carla stole my new watch, and she won't give it back. Make her give it to me, please."

"Now wait a minute, Patty," Miss Bear said. "You must be very certain about this. It would be terribly wrong to accuse Carla of stealing your watch if she didn't."

"But she must have," Patty argued. "She was in the washroom at noon, and that's when I missed mine. And now she is wearing one just like it. She must have taken it."

But when Miss Bear called Carla in for an explanation, the girl still told the same story she had told before.

"I know it is just like Patty's," she insisted. "That is why I was so proud of it. I thought Patty was the nicest girl in the whole room and I wanted to be just like her. When I opened my present at noon, I was so happy that I had a watch like hers."

"We shall have to let this go until we can get to the bottom of it," Miss Bear decided.

"I have no right to take the watch away from Carla," she told Patty, "so you will just have to wait until tomorrow morning. By that time perhaps we shall know more about this."

Patty could hardly wait to get home and tell her mother about the loss of the watch and about the new girl who had envied it enough to steal it from her.

She burst into the house, crying, "Mother, Mother, do you know what happened?" But she could not find her mother anywhere. When she reached her room, she found a note on her dresser that read: "Patty, I have gone to see Mrs. Anderson. I will be back before five."

Patty hung up her coat and changed into her play clothes. She went into the bathroom to get a drink of water, and there on the side of the washbowl lay her watch, its beautiful gold case glinting brightly in the slanting afternoon sun!

Patty was speechless, and a slow flush crept up her neck and burned its way into her cheeks. Her stomach tied up in a hard ball of shame. She remembered now washing the peanut butter off her fingers before she went back to school at lunch time. And she had laid her watch there while she washed. It was yesterday that she had placed it on the window sill at school —and she had said those awful things about Carla! And Carla was probably at home now, crying and crying.

Patty snatched up her yellow scarf and dashed out of the house and down the street in the direction of Carla's house. Thank goodness, she knew where Carla lived!

It took courage to knock on the door of the brown house set way back from the street. Patty was out of breath, and her face still burned at the thought of how she had treated this little stranger in their school.

Carla herself came to the door, her eyes red with weeping, her left arm bare of any watch.

Patty did not wait for Carla to speak.

"Oh, Carla, I am so ashamed; I found my watch at home after all. Martha tried to tell me I shouldn't accuse anyone of taking it until I was sure. But I thought I was sure —" She fumbled for words in embarrassment. "Will you — can you ever forgive me?"

"It's all right," Carla said hesitatingly as she wiped her eyes. "Now I can wear my watch again. I put it away because I just couldn't stand to wear it." She rubbed her bare wrist.

"It's not all right yet," Patty said. "I accused you in front of Miss Bear and the other girls. I will have to tell them all how wrong I was."

And Patty did tell them; though it was the hardest thing she had ever done. As soon as all the boys and girls were settled at their desks the next morning, she raised her hand for permission to speak. When Miss Bear nodded her consent, Patty stood up in front of them all. Her eyes stung, and she felt as though she were going to cry. She swallowed twice and began very slowly.

"I did something that was terribly wrong yesterday," she said. "I accused Carla of taking my watch when I wasn't really sure. When I got home, I found mine on the washbowl where I had left it."

She glanced at Carla. The happy relief in Carla's shining eyes gave her courage to go on. She continued in a surer voice.

"Carla told me last night she would forgive me, and I will never be so quick to think wrong of anyone again."

"It is good of Carla to forgive you so quickly," said Miss Bear. "And you are brave and courageous to admit before the class that you have made a mistake. I know we shall all profit by your example."

As Patty took her seat, the warm glow on Carla's face was reflected in her own light heart, and she knew that in righting the wrong, she had gained a new friend.

TINNY, TIN, TIN*

Laura S. Emerson

The missionary and his wife bounced over the jungle road in their truck. It was a privilege to carry the true gospel story to a tribe which had never yet heard this message. Their two children gazed curiously around, listening to the tales of the native helper with them. They were traveling through the game area of Equatorial East Africa where rhinos, lions, and elephants abounded.

A tremendous downpour of tropical rain compelled them to stop in the middle of the afternoon. Drenched to the skin, as the rain continued to fall, they set up camp and prepared for a much-needed rest.

About midnight, the missionary was suddenly awakened. He felt a strange motion. The ground under him seemed to be moving — rising and lowering in perfect rhythm. He heard the snap of twigs and the swish, swish of some large animal walking through the tall elephant-grass which surrounded the frail tent. As he lay there, he realized that if a large rhino were approaching, it would pass right through the tent and kill them all.

Quietly the missionary rolled from his cot, picked up his rifle, and slipped noiselessly through the flaps of the tent. The rain had ceased. The little clearing was bathed in brilliant, tropical moonlight which enabled him to see everything clearly. There was nothing directly in front of him.

With his finger on the trigger, he cautiously peeped around the corner, ready for action. To his surprise, just twenty-three steps away from him stood, not one, but two, five, ten, yes, fifteen huge elephants! The herd had been coming in single file, head to tail. When they saw the camp, they stopped to look it over. As soon as they sensed his presence, they lifted their trunks into the air and trumpeted as they always do before a stampede.

On sudden impulse, the missionary raised his gun to fire at the first elephant. Then his better judgment checked him. He knew

*A true experience of Rev. Robert K. Smith, Missionary of *World Gospel Mission.* Used by permission.

161

that if he were to hit each beast with every shot in his magazine, there would still be enough elephants to destroy his camp and all his loved ones!

There was only a moment to act! What should he do?

How could the missionary know that in America, 12,000 miles away from him, but close enough to talk with God, a faithful Christian lady was washing windows in her home. As she worked, her Heavenly Father asked her to stop and pray for this missionary and his family in far away Africa. She was so busy just then. She hesitated. But God lovingly showed her that they were in grave danger. Just where she was, she knelt down and poured out her heart to God, asking Him to protect the missionaries, to deliver them from danger, and to spare their lives. God heard her cry, and lifted the burden. She was so impressed that she wrote down the time on her calendar before she continued her window-washing.

But the elephants were nearly upon the missionary! There was no time to warn his family. In his confusion, he stumbled backward. Stepping blindly, he unintentionally bumped the table upon which were stacked the tin cooking utensils. To his horror, the table tipped over with a metallic crash, scattering the pots and pans with a loud clatter! Thinking that all was lost, the missionary looked up to see the elephant herd slide to a stop. They lifted their trunks high in air and trumpeted loudly again. Throwing their trunks down, and their heads back into line, the whole herd turned and marched angrily away in double-quick time. They pushed over trees, and rolled rocks down the hillside as they crashed back across the clearing into the jungle.

The next morning the missionary and his party broke camp and went on into the country of the tribe to whom they were to minister. One day an ivory-hunter visited the camp. After the missionary had told him of their midnight elephant experience, the old hunter said, "You did the only known thing that will frighten away elephants. Beat on a pan or a piece of tin and they will always run. Shoot at them and they will always charge!"

Although the missionary had not known this, God had! He it was who whispered to the working woman to stop to pray for their deliverance. It was God who caused the missionary to dump all the tin in camp on the ground. It was God who turned the elephants about and enabled the missionary to proclaim His power to another African tribe.

THE SHEPHERD*

William MacKellar

Wee Sandy peered out of the tiny window. The nearby Scottish mountains seemed to have vanished in the gloom and in the swirling snow.

"It's myself is glad I'm no' out on the hills this night," he said thankfully.

His father laid down the Bible he was reading and nodded.

"Aye, 'tis an ill night, Sandy. And 'tis grand we have a warm fire and a strong thatched roof over us." He paused and placed a peat block in the glowing flames. "But there will be one man out on the hills tonight, I'm thinking. That will be the Reverend Mr. MacTavish."

"The minister?" asked Sandy in surprise. "And why should he be out in the hills on such a night, now?" He turned his gaze once again at the bleak scene through the window. A tiny shiver of fear ran through him at the great emptiness outside.

"Because old Mrs. Grant will be expecting him, laddie. 'Tis an ill woman she is and dearly loves the Word. So you will be understanding why the minister must go to her. A grand man he is," concluded Sandy's father simply.

The young Highland boy looked at him in astonishment. "Does the minister have a warm fire like this?"

"Aye, Sandy, he does."

"And a strong thatched roof like we have?"

"Aye."

Wee Sandy stared. "And he goes out on a night like this to visit an old woman? 'Tis a daft fool he is, I'm thinking."

An understanding smile claimed his father's face. When he spoke, his voice was soft with a deep gentleness. "I'm thinking it's the Lord Himself that needs more daft fools like the Reverend Mr. MacTavish, Sandy. Aye, it —" He never finished the sentence. Someone was pounding loudly on the door.

"Now who would that be on such a night?" he muttered. He drew up the heavy crossbar on the door. A snow-draped figure staggered into the room. It was Jock Brown, their nearest neighbor.

"Your sheep are out!" cried Jock breathlessly. His chest rose and fell as though with exhaustion. "The wind has taken away

*Reprinted from *Stories to Tell Boys and Girls*. Used with permission.

a part of your sheepfold, and there's some of them out on the hills!"

Wee Sandy stared at his father. Well he knew what it meant to lose the sheep. But surely his father wouldn't dare go out after them on a night like this.

The boy's father gave a soft, low whistle. In an instant Bruce, the great collie was by his side.

"I'm going out after the sheep, Sandy," he said. He drew on his heavy coat and picked up a lantern. "Put on some hot tea for later."

"May I come?" asked Sandy.

His father paused at the door which Jock Brown was already opening. "You?" he said. "A wee laddie like you, Sandy?" He stepped out into the snow. "Don't forget the hot tea." The door slammed behind him.

Alone in the house Sandy could hear the wind. It moaned around the windows. It wailed down the chimney. Sandy couldn't remember such a horrible night. He felt a little frightened as he boiled the water for the tea. What a night!

Then quite suddenly there was a lull — a deep calm, as though all the winds in Scotland were gathering for one huge, final puff. In the stillness Sandy heard the cry quite clearly.

"Baa —"   His heart skipped a beat. One of the sheep was close to the cottage!

Drawing on his boots and heavy coat he rushed out into the storm. His feet sank in the deep drifts; the wind was icy cold against his skin. Around him the snow swirled madly. It stung his eyes so that he could not lift his head to see around him.

"Hallo-o-o!" he yelled. "Hallo-o-o!" He waited, but there was no answering cry. Only the wail of the wind rushing through the night.

"Hallo-o-o!" he cried again. "Hallo-o-o!" Again he waited. Again there was no answer. Sandy tried to remember from what point the sheep's cry had come. But it was hard to tell with the blinding snow. He gritted his teeth and continued his search. Twenty minutes later he knew he was lost.

Sandy was frightened. The friendly light from the cottage was gone. Darkness was all around him. He couldn't tell where he was. And his knee had begun to hurt after he had fallen into that last snowdrift.

"Baa —"   Sandy jumped and stared down at his feet. He had almost stepped on a small, black-nosed Highland sheep!

With a glad shout Sandy threw his arms around the poor animal. Tenderly he lifted it from the drift in which it had lain.

Its long fleece was heavy with ice, and it gave a pitiful little cry as he held it in his arms.

"It's all right now," said Sandy to his little woolly burden. "It's all right now."

But it wasn't. When Sandy tried to walk, he gave a sharp cry of pain. His knee had swollen badly, and it hurt just to put his foot on the ground. Limping painfully, he made his way through the ever deepening snow. If he only knew where the cottage was!

Slowly Sandy felt his strength leave him. Grimly clutching the sheep, he slid down against a tree. He could go no further. It seemed hours later that a huge figure suddenly loomed out of the snow.

Wee Sandy tried to call out. He was so weak by this time that the wind seemed to freeze his faint cry while it was yet in his throat. But the man must have heard. Suddenly Sandy felt a pair of great hands pick him up gently. And that was the last that Sandy remembered until he woke up in the cottage.

"Sandy!" His father was standing over him on the couch. "Thank God you're all right, laddie." He turned to the man who had found and carried his son home. "And it was the Lord, too, who guided your steps this night, Mr. MacTavish. But why the laddie went out I'll never know."

"I heard the sheep calling," said Sandy. He could feel his strength returning slowly. "It was myself just had to go. For it's right that I should be a shepherd like my father, is it not, Mr. MacTavish?"

The minister smiled. "Of course, Sandy. A shepherd has to watch his sheep. And when they call to him, he just has to go."

Sandy nodded. "I heard it crying. It seemed to be crying just to me." He paused. Something still troubled him, though. He looked curiously at the minister. "I'm right glad you found me, Mr. MacTavish. But 'tis myself can't understand —" He stopped, not sure how to go on.

"Why I was out there, too?" the minister said.

Sandy nodded. "Aye," he said.

"It's because I'm a shepherd too, Sandy. Not exactly like you, but a shepherd just the same. I have a flock too, the people of my parish. And when I hear them calling me, like old Mrs. Grant did tonight, I have to go." He put his arm very gently around the boy's shoulder. "You understand, don't you?"

Wee Sandy smiled and nodded. He felt proud that he was a shepherd. Like his father. Like the minister. "Aye," he said, "I understand now."

GUEST OF HONOR*

Grace V. Watkins

With more speed than his seventy years would warrant, Professor Timothy Dunn hustled into his academic robes and walked briskly across the campus. No use letting anyone think he was getting old, even if this was his last commencement as a faculty member. No use getting sentimental about it, either! It was going to be fun to retire and do all the things he hadn't found time for during his forty-two years at Bainbury! Beautiful morning! Commencement was always more meaningful with bright sunlight streaming across the green lawns and resting warmly on the campus buildings.

"Prof. D." (he liked that nickname!) adjusted his mortarboard with an experienced hand, rounded the corner of Old Main, and made his way past the chattering seniors to the ranks of somewhat more dignified faculty and trustees. Glancing toward the head of the line, he spied a distinguished-looking man talking with President Marlowe — guest of honor for the day, no doubt — Bainbury's most famous alumnus, John Douglas Hamilton — lecturer, world traveler, author — here to receive an honorary degree. How well Prof. D. remembered him from the old days—a gangly, redheaded youngster from a nearby farm who delivered laundry and waited tables and mowed faculty lawns to finance his way through college. "Johnny Ham" he was called in that long-gone era.

"Wonder if he'd remember his old English teacher," the professor asked himself and was instantly ashamed of coveting a spark of reflected glory.

Organ music sounded from the chapel. Slowly the procession circled the campus, calm and stately as a river on a June morning. A colorful sight! Something within Prof. D. always rose as if on wings when he saw the bright velvet and satin hoods. Universities all over the country were represented. A little college was Bainbury, yet its faculty came from far places!

Sitting in the faculty section of the audience, Prof. D. (though he wouldn't have admitted it to anyone!) found his eyes turning

*Reprinted from *The Christian Herald* and used by permission of the author.

166

to the guest of honor seated on the platform with the other
dignitaries. Suddenly Prof. D. remembered a long-gone September morning, an awkward freshman, wide-eyed, a little frightened, standing beside an English professor's desk, face shining.
"You see, Sir," the words came back vividly, "I want to write. I
want it more than anything in the world, but I don't know if I'm
good enough or ever will be. It's all I care about. I've thought
about it when I was plowing corn and when I was feeding pigs,
and really all the time, I guess."

Then Prof. D. heard his own voice saying, "The thing we
want to do is usually the thing we do best. But remember, son,
it's a long road and a hard one; it will mean years of study and
toil, and a lot of discouragement. The world needs good writers,
though, and I hope you'll be one of them."

On the platform the guest of honor shifted in his chair —
suave, poised man of letters, two best-sellers to his credit already,
a political novel, *Journey into Freedom,* coming out in a few
weeks. Bored stiff, no doubt, by the puny pomp and ceremony of
a little, church-related college in a small town among quiet hills.
Looking only half interested in what the speaker of the morning
was saying. Probably thinking about how soon he could catch
the next train back to New York. What did John Douglas Hamilton care about Bainbury after all these years of tasting fame in
the capitals of the world. Silly to have invited him here!

Prof. D. indulged in a bit of self-pity. That's the way it went
— you gave the best years of your life to a small college and
what thanks did you get? Maybe he would have been better off
in a larger institution — more prestige and all that. But somehow
Bainbury had been a symbol to him — a symbol of faith and
goodness and truth, like a shrine, something stirring his heart
and challenging his spirit as though a clear sweet call drifted
from far high altars. A call to spend his days in the shadow of
the church, to follow the mellow campus paths, to walk the
quiet hills; and in his corner classroom to give undergraduates
what he liked to call "learning plus," a certain inner light, a
sense of enduring values, which he hoped would remain with
them always; as though they had walked through quiet aisles
where white candles were burning. That was the glory of the
small church-related college, Prof. D. deflected. He sighed.
Johnny Ham had probably forgotten all of this.

The speaker finished his predictions of things to come in the
realm of higher education, and the seniors filed across the plat-

form to receive their degrees — the radiance of long expectation and now fulfillment on their faces.

Now President Marlowe was drawing himself up to his full dignity and turning toward the waiting audience, a paternal smile on his scholarly face. This is it, Prof. D. told himself. He was gratified to notice that Johnny Ham looked halfway interested.

"And now," began the president, "it is my privilege and my pleasure to bestow upon one of Bainbury's most distinguished sons an honor of which he is eminently deserving." President Marlowe turned toward the candidate. The famous man of letters rose. The audience sat motionless.

"John Douglas Hamilton," the president continued, "writer, student of world affairs, interpreter of present-day events, distinguished son of Bainbury, in recognition of the service you have rendered the current age, and the honor you have brought to your alma mater, by authority of the trustees of this institution, I now confer upon you the degree of Doctor of Literature, with all the rights and privileges thereunto appertaining, in token of which the hood to be placed upon your shoulders shall forever be a symbol."

Bainbury's greatest alumnus stood quietly while Dean Orringer, with careful precision, arranged the gold-and-crimson hood on his shoulders. Prof. D. clapped loudly with the rest of the audience. After the ceremonies he'd look Johnny Ham up, introduce himself and offer congratulations. Even if the great man didn't remember him, it would be a courteous thing to do.

Why didn't the "honored son" sit down? Prof. D. stirred restlessly. He was getting tired. Then, to his surprise, the famous man began to speak and strangely enough, not at all in the cool, well-modulated voice Prof. D. would have expected.

"My dear friends," he said, "to return in this way to a well-loved place is a great joy and a great privilege. The four years at Bainbury were a rich experience, in some ways the best years of my life. For them I shall always be deeply grateful.

"I come to you from far places — places in which there is pain and grief and suffering beyond anything which this fortunate and peaceful valley has ever known. Be glad for the blessings which you possess. Be proud of Bainbury College. It is giving you and your children a priceless heritage, an unsullied vision, as it gave them to me.

"Today I have been honored by my alma mater. I speak from

the depths of my heart when I say I have never received a greater honor or one which made me more humble.

"But there is another whom Bainbury honors today, and upon whom an honorary degree is to be conferred." Prof. D. fumbled with his program. He couldn't find any other name listed.

"No," the speaker continued, "you won't find his name on the program. Yet you all know him and love him. He is your friend and mine.

"One day, years ago, when I was sitting in a college English class, we read a work of literature. I can't remember now what it was, but there was a passage about freedom. The professor said to us, 'Always remember — freedom is not a possession, but a journey.' It was then that the title of my new book, soon to be published, was born. It happened at Bainbury, and the professor was Timothy Fuller Dunn. *He* is your guest of honor today. He will be escorted to the platform by Professor Blake and Professor Nolan."

Prof. D's heart gave a mighty leap! They *couldn't* mean him! Yet here came the two professors beckoning him to the aisle, taking him by the arms, walking with him to the platform. Unbelievingly he looked at the president and at the beautiful hood which was brought from behind the curtains. His knees trembled.

The president began to speak. "Timothy Fuller Dunn, beloved citizen of Bainbury, inspiring teacher, wise counselor, loyal friend, faithful steward of the Kingdom, by the authority vested in me by the trustees of this institution, I now confer upon you the degree of Doctor of Literature, with all the rights and privileges thereunto appertaining, of which the hood to be placed on your shoulders shall forever be a symbol."

It was never quite clear to Prof. D. what happened then. After the beautiful gold-and-crimson hood became his own, there was a thunder of applause, handshaking, words of appreciation, faces lighted with love and pride. Then after the commencement luncheon, somehow he and Johnny Ham were walking across the campus arm in arm, then talking earnestly in the old classroom, and later, waiting at the station so that Johnny could catch the train back to New York.

When the train had rounded the curve behind Blackberry Hill and disappeared from sight, Prof. D. walked slowly up the small street where the afternoon sunlight lay like gold.

"Yes," he said to himself, "this is where I belonged all these years. I wouldn't change one day of it," and he thought of the closing lines of a poem he had read long ago:

> A college is longing and laughter,
> And fear and fulfillment,
> And looking forward,
> And looking back.
> A college goes on forever,
> Not in microscopes or maps
> Or ledgers or violins,
> Or even tall maples that brush the sky,
> But in the still reaches of the hearts
> That having loved it
> And afterward understood it,
> Bear its mark forever.

VICTORY THROUGH SONG*

Laura S. Emerson

Three dollars! That was the amount Martha needed before the first of the month, which was only eight days away. Ever since the Rev. Allen Black, a returned missionary from Mexico, had spoken to her Sunday school about the little, dark-faced Mexican children who needed Bibles in their own Spanish language, she had wanted to help. When her class of junior girls had made pledges, Martha had promised three dollars. All offerings were to be paid a week from Sunday. This was Saturday!

Again Martha counted her savings: the quarter Aunt Lois had given her for the "A" on her report card, fifty cents from Mrs. Jones for taking care of Betty, and two dimes and a nickel carefully hoarded from her small weekly allowances. All in all, it totalled only one dollar, not three. She so loved her little leather-bound Bible that she wanted those Mexican girls to have Bibles of their own, too.

Her thoughts were interrupted by her mother's voice, as she asked her to go on an errand to the drugstore downtown. Martha went gladly. She liked to mingle with the Saturday shoppers, but this morning she paid little attention to those she passed as she hurried on.

How could she get two more dollars? She knew Uncle Charlie would give it to her, but her teacher had said a gift must be a part of the giver! So she did not want to ask him. Walking along Main Street, she wrestled with her problem.

Then, right in front of the dime store, she noticed a small, black coin purse on the edge of the sidewalk! She reached down and picked it up. No one seemed to notice her among the busy shoppers. She stepped in front of a store entrance and opened the purse. A green bill caught her eye, only one, but, oh, it was a twenty-dollar bill! Her eyes gleamed! Twenty dollars! Why, she could pay her pledge and still have eighteen dollars left. Was that all? There were some car keys, a bankbook, and a

*Reprinted from *The Sunday School Times* and used by permission.

171

little change. Quickly Martha closed the purse and continued on her errand.

Twenty dollars! Twenty dollars! But was it hers? This new thought troubled her, and her steps lagged. This problem was bigger than her need. She passed the drugstore before she realized it and walked around the city block, fighting her battle. No one had seen her find the purse; she wanted the money for others, for a good cause, not for herself. Never had she been so tempted; never had that subtle voice seemed so loud in her ear. Then an old, familiar song came to her mind:

> Yield not to temptation,
> For yielding is sin. . . .

She hummed the chorus aloud:

> Ask the Saviour to help you,
> Comfort, strengthen, and keep you;
> He is willing to aid you,
> He will carry you through.

"Dear Jesus, do help me!" She breathed the prayer from her heart. How clear it all seemed now! Why, it would be — yes, it would be *stealing* to take what didn't belong to her if she made no attempt to find the owner.

Stepping into the bank entrance, she opened the purse once more. That must be the owner's name on the bankbook — Mrs. J. C. Blake. Why, the book was from the State Bank. That was where she was now. Oh, she mustn't listen to that tempting voice another minute!

She opened the heavy bank door and stood in the short line before the first window. Soon she was telling the cashier her story.

"Do you know Mrs. Blake?" she asked.

"Yes, she is one of our customers," he replied. "We'll be glad to get in touch with her today."

With relief she handed him the purse; it burned in her pocket.

"Thank you for returning this," she heard him say. "What is your name? Mrs. Blake will want to know."

Martha wrote down her address, then hurried to the drugstore and started homeward. How lighthearted she felt, knowing that she had done right! Somehow she knew that the Lord would help her solve her other problem, too. She sang her song on the way home.

When Martha returned from school five days later, her mother told her that she had received a registered letter that afternoon. She opened it hurriedly, wondering who would be writing to her. Three crisp dollar bills fell out of the envelope. Who could be sending her money? The brief note was signed by Mrs. J. C. Blake. Blake? Who was Mrs. Blake? Oh, the owner of the bankbook! The banker had told her about the little girl, and she wanted to reward Martha.

"Oh, see, Mother!" she called. "Now I can pay my Mexican pledge this Sunday, and I'll have one dollar besides!"

She looked at the bills again. These were really hers. She had a right to keep them. What if she had not listened to the song! Jesus did help me — He brought victory through a song, she thought, as she went upstairs to her room joyfully singing:

> Look ever to Jesus,
> He'll carry you through.

BIBLIOGRAPHY

I. TECHNIQUE OF STORYTELLING

BROWN, JEANETTE PERKINS. *The Story Teller in Religious Education.* Boston: The Pilgrim Press, 1951.

ROYAL, CLAUDIA. *Storytelling.* Nashville, Tennessee: Broadman Press, 1955.

SAWYER, RUTH. *The Way of the Story-Teller.* New York: Viking Press, 1947.

SHEDLOCK, MARIE. *The Art of the Story-Teller.* New York: Dover Publications, Inc., 1952.

(Out of print texts still available in libraries)

BAILEY, CAROLYN. For the Story-Teller. Springfield, Massachusetts: Milton Bradley Co., 1930.

BRYANT, SARA CONE. *How to Tell Stories to Children.* New York: Houghton Mifflin Co., 1933.

CATHER, KATHERINE DUNLAP. *Religious Education Through Story-Telling.* Nashville, Tennessee: Abingdon Press, 1925.

EGGLESTON, MARGARET. *Use of the Story in 'Religious Education.* New York: Harper & Brothers, Pub., 1936.

ESENWEIN, J. BERG, and STOCKARD, MARIETTA. *Children's Stories and How to Tell Them.* Springfield, Massachusetts: The Home Correspondence School, 1917.

II. PAMPHLETS

FOR THE STORYTELLER. National Recreation Association, 315 Fourth Avenue, New York 10, N. Y., 1952.

STORYTELLING. National Recreation Association, 8 W. Eighth Street, New York 11, N. Y., 1938.

STORY ART MAGAZINE. Official organ of the National Story League, Box 9827, Dallas 14, Texas.

III. ABOUT BOOKS AND STORIES

ADAMS, BESS PORTER. *About Books and Children.* New York: Henry Holt & Co., 1953.

ARBUTHNOT, MAY HILL. *Children and Books.* New York: Scott, Foresman & Co., Revised Edition, 1957.

DUFF, ANNIS. *Bequest of Wings.* New York: Viking Press, 1946.

EATON, ANNE T. *Reading with Children.* New York: Viking Press, 1940.

IV. ANTHOLOGIES OF STORIES

ARBUTHNOT, MAY HILL. *The Arbuthnot Anthology.* Chicago: Scott, Foresman & Co., 1952.

HUBER, MIRIAM BLANTON. *Story and Verse for Children.* New York: Macmillan, 1955.

JOHNSON, EDNA, SCOTT, CARRIE and SICKELS, EVELYN. *Anthology of Children's Literature.* Houghton Mifflin Co., 1948.

GOODMAN, ROBERT (ed.). *Masterpieces for Radio and Declamation.* New York: Liberty Publishing Co., Liberty Square, 1943.

MALONE, TED. *Favorite Stories.* Garden City, New York: Doubleday & Co., Inc., 1950.

V. COLLECTIONS FOR RELIGIOUS EDUCATORS

BAILEY, FAITH COXE. *Tales for Teens.* Chicago: Moody Press.

BRYANT, AL (ed.). *Stories to Tell Boys and Girls.* Grand Rapids, Michigan: Zondervan Publishing House.

EGERMEIER, ELSIE. *Boy's Stories of Great Men.* Anderson, Indiana: The Warner Press, 1931.

———. *Girl's Stories of Great Women.* Anderson, Indiana: The Warner Press, 1930.

EGGLESTON, MARGARET. *Thirty Stories I Like to Tell.* New York: Harper & Brothers Publishers, 1949.

———. *Forty Stories for Church, School, and Home.* New York: Harper & Brothers Publishers, 1939.

EMERSON, LAURA S. *25 Inspiring Readings.* Kansas City, Missouri: Lillenas Publishing Co., 1952.

HAGEDORN, HERMAN. *The Book of Courage.* Winston, 1930.

MILLEN, NINA. *The Missionary Story Hour.* New York: Friendship Press, 1952.

———. *Missionary Hero Stories.* New York: Friendship Press, 1948.

MILLER, BASIL. *Ten Boys Who Became Famous.* (8 Vols. in "10 Famous" Series). Grand Rapids, Michigan: Zondervan Publishing House.

———. *Ten Girls Who Became Famous.* Grand Rapids, Michigan: Zondervan Publishing House.

PEALE, NORMAN VINCENT. *Guidepost Anthology.* New York: Prentice-Hall, Inc., 1953, (annual).

TAYLOR, KENNETH. *Stories for the Children's Hour.* Chicago: Moody Press.

TURNBULL, AGNES S. *Far Above Rubies.* New York: Fleming H. Revell Co., 1926.

VI. STORY-TELLING RECORDS

American Library Association, 50 East Huron St., Chicago, Illinois.

SAWYER, RUTH. "The Frog."

SAYERS, FRANCES CLARK. "Br'er Mud Turtle's Trickery."

THORNE-THOMSEN, GUNDRUN. "Gudbrand-on-the-Hillside."

Audio Bible Society of America, Inc., 1061 Memorial Ave., Williamsport, Pennsylvania.

Barrett, Ethel. The Children's Library.

Caldmon Publishers, 277 Fifth Avenue, New York 16, New York.

SCHILDKRAUT, JOSEPH. "Grimm Fairy Tales."

Educational Service, Radio Corporation of America, Camden, New Jersey.

LAUGHTON, CHARLES. Reading from the Bible. "Fiery Furnace."

———. "Noah's Ark."

TEMPLETON, ALEC. "The Pied Piper of Hamlin."

Index

INDEX

179